A PRACTICAL GUIDE TO
DIVERSIFICATION FOR CARE HOMES

Jenyth Worsley

© 1995 Jenyth Worsley
Published by Age Concern England
1268 London Road
London SW16 4ER

Editor Gillian Clarke
Design and typesetting Eugenie Dodd Typographics
Production Andrew Clifford
Copy preparation Vinnette Marshall
Printed and bound in Great Britain by Bell & Bain Ltd, Glasgow

A catalogue record for this book is available from the British Library.

ISBN 0–86242–154–3

Contents

About the Author

Expanding Care is the third book that Jenyth Worsley has written for Age Concern England: she is also the author of *Taking Good Care: A handbook for care assistants* and *Good Care Management: A guide to setting up and managing a residential home.* Other subjects she has written about include the performing arts, negotiation skills, working in nursing and teaching for the Careers and Occupational Department of the Department of Employment. She has also contributed articles on music and the women's movement for the *Oxford Children's Encyclopedia,* published by the Oxford University Press.

Jenyth earlier worked in the BBC as a producer and writer in education and drama. In 1992 she co-founded Writers in Oxford. She is now writing and performing her own poetry, and in 1994 was a semi finalist in the BBC Radio 4 'Speak a Poem' competition.

Acknowledgements

I should like to express my gratitude and appreciation to the following people and organisations for their help in the preparation of this book.

First, my thanks go to Martin Bradshaw, Commissioning Officer in the Social Services Department of Oxfordshire County Council, for his initial advice and contacts, for his speedy reading of the manuscript in various stages and for his suggested amendments and improvements at each stage. I also acknowledge the help of Dr Roger Morgan of the Independent Inspection Unit and of Oxfordshire Social Services Department for allowing me to quote from their contracts and directives.

My special thanks go to Barbara and Ross Greig of Fairholme House, Bodicote, for their informative advice and comments and for giving me access to their own research and records, and to William Bowley, Chairman of the Oxfordshire Care Association.

Thanks are also due to Hilary Goodrich and Delia Styles of the Oxfordshire Health Authority, Dame Cicely Saunders of St Christopher's Hospice and David Wolverson of Anchor Housing Association, which has allowed one to quote from their Philosophy of Care.

Charles Hardy has allowed the use of his concept of the Sigmoid Curve. Sheila Scott, Chief Executive of the National Care Homes Association, and Christabel Shawcross, at the Department of Health Social Services Inspectorate, gave valuable suggestions for the completed manuscript.

From Age Concern England, I am grateful to Evelyn McEwen and Lorna Easterbrook for their perceptive comments, to Gillian Clarke for her capable steering of the project throughout, and to Vinnette Marshall for keying it all in.

Jenyth Worsley

Preface

Over the last few years, profound changes have taken place in our society that have affected the way we work, our home life and our social attitudes and expectations. The reasons are complex: economic recession, government policy, developments in communications and information technology have all played their part. As a result almost everyone is having to face a lack of stability in their lives and find a way of coming to terms with change.

Change can be regarded as frightening, or a challenge, or something that need not happen until it is absolutely necessary. The person who likes a challenge often rushes into change without assessing how best to proceed. The wait-and-see person often waits until it is too late. Owners of residential and nursing Homes who foresaw in 1990 where community care was leading have a head start on others who are only just considering it now.

This book is about the pitfalls and possibilities of change for the owner or manager of a care Home. It expresses the views and experience of Home owners, employees in local authorities (including the inspectorate and planning units), relatives, carers and older people themselves. Each has a different perspective and has something of value to contribute. And, as the problem of diversifying a core business is not unique to the care sector, the book also includes the views of people in industry and management training who are concerned with the wider implications of change within our society.

How to Use the Book

The book gives both background information and practical advice. As the circumstances of individual Homes will be very different, you will need to determine which is most useful for you. The opening chapter looks at the current market for residential and domiciliary care and discusses the new roles of the local authorities in the purchase and provision of care.

Chapter 2, Taking Stock, gives advice on how to look at the business from all angles, so that you are in a position to take informed decisions.

Chapters 3 and 4 suggest the ways in which you can diversify, either from the Home, which would remain as your core business, or by changing completely the nature of the establishment.

Chapters 5, 6 and 7 give practical suggestions on the business and marketing side.

Chapter 8 provides a set of checklists to work through before taking the final steps needed to change a business and Appendix 1 outlines the procedures involved if you decide to close the Home.

1 Setting the Scene

In the 1990s, most owners and managers of care Homes for older people have found that they need to consider carefully what their options are in terms of making the best use of their resources and skills. This book aims to provide guidance in assessing whether it is possible to diversify and develop the business of a Home, the steps you will need to take in order to make it successful, or whether the most realistic option is to close down. Although this book is designed primarily for Home owners in the independent sector, the suggestions given may also be helpful for those managing local authority Homes.

THE CURRENT SITUATION

In the last ten years two major factors have affected care for older people: the 1990 NHS and Community Care Act and the housing boom of the 1980s which was followed by recession. Under the Act, which came fully into force in 1993, money which the Department of Social Security (DSS) used to pay directly to people in residential or nursing Homes in the form of Income Support has been transferred to local authorities as a Special Transitional Grant (STG). Local authorities have a legal responsibility to pay for residential care for older people who qualify on grounds of income and capital and whom they have assessed as needing such care. Each authority decides independently how much is to be spent on residential care and how much should be spent on care within the community. Older people who were living permanently in private or voluntary Homes when the Act was passed have the right to protected funding from the DSS. For those who want to understand this Act in detail, *The Community Care*

Handbook by Barbara Meredith, published by Age Concern England (see p 139), is essential reading.

The role of the local authority

Now that the 1990 Act has come into force, it is easier to assess its effects in a number of areas:

- the role of the local authority in the purchase and provision of community care
- how community care is funded
- how people are assessed as needing different levels of care
- where this care is provided – in a residential Home or in the individual's own home.

The new Act has altered dramatically the role and responsibilities of local authorities in how they provide and arrange or oversee care. Each authority will have had a number of residential care Homes ('Part III' Homes) which they ran without any input from the private or voluntary sector. In the independent sector, often the only time a residential Home owner met anyone other than a social worker from the local authority was during the twice-yearly inspection – which was independent from the social services department (SSD). It is probably fair to say that both sides have at times been suspicious of the attitudes and practices of the other.

The 1990 Act has brought together the independent sector and the local authorities in a new way. Care boundaries themselves are changing: both nursing and residential Homes are taking on each other's roles and/or clients through dual registration, which is likely to increase. At least two health authorities have contracted out inspection of nursing Homes to the local authority inspectors. There is a feeling among professional social service workers that the registration for residential and nursing homes may merge within the next few years. This would mean that a Home could offer the most appropriate form of care for an older person, including nursing by nursing staff, and that registration would be for different levels, which could include personal and nursing care. Private agencies, who may offer an all-inclusive domiciliary care service, may be able to offer this sort of flexibility for an individual.

However, this is for the future. Under the current legislation, local authorities:

- Are encouraged to become *enablers* and *purchasers* rather than solely *providers* (see Glossary at the end of the book).

- Are responsible for the *registration* of independent Homes (by the 'arm's length' inspection and registration unit) and for the inspection of all residential Homes in the area, including their own Part III Homes.

- Are encouraged to make full use of the independent sector (not necessarily popular in political terms).

- Have many more responsibilities for deciding and arranging or providing assessment (after consultation) for the most appropriate type of care for each individual.

The role of health authorities and GP fund-holders

The Department of Health (DoH) is currently reviewing NHS responsibilities for people with long-term social and health care needs. These will include the purchase of packages of care from providers in the public and independent sectors. Different models of care may be appropriate in different parts of the country. The DoH has stressed the importance of close collaboration of health authorities and GPs with local authorities on a number of issues. These include:

- hospital discharge of people with long-term care needs

- care of older people suffering from dementia

- care of older people with other medical, nursing, psychiatric or other assessed specialist needs.

New patterns of services are likely to evolve, and health authorities must make sure that people know who is eligible and how they are assessed. Details of services and health authorities should be published in the local Community Care Plans (see below).

The Community Care Plan

Every local authority is required by law to draw up a Community Care Plan, which is published each year after local consultation with district or regional health authorities and housing authorities as well as with voluntary sector groups and private individuals.

Community Care Plans can be complex documents, sometimes up to 100 pages long. However, they are designed to be read by the general public, so they should be easy to follow. A Community Care Plan is the blueprint for all future care in your area. It will include:

- the needs for care
- current services
- the changes that may be required in future developments of care in the community
- plans for the next financial year.

Every Plan is a continuing dialogue on the development of services with voluntary organisations, users and carers, the independent sector and the local people.

The Community Care Plan also states the principles on which the authority operates in providing care. For example, the following are some extracts from the Oxfordshire Community Care Plan.

- All services should be of the highest quality, underpinned by training and monitoring systems. They should be aimed at meeting each individual's right to maximum physical, mental and emotional well-being.
- Services and treatments should be designed to promote independence. They should be aimed at allowing people to live at home as far as possible, and at ensuring that stays in hospital are as short as possible, bearing in mind the need for adequate aftercare and rehabilitation.
- In some cases, residential, nursing care or sheltered housing may be the right and preferred option.
- People should be party to and able to influence decisions about their lives.

Several departments of local authorities are involved in putting into effect both the 1990 Community Care Act and the 1984 Registered Homes Act. A brief survey of their individual responsibilities is given below.

The local authority inspection and registration unit

Under the 1990 Community Care Act, this 'arm's length' unit has the responsibility for *inspecting* and *registering* residential Homes for children and for adults. The whole range includes Homes for children, for elderly people, for adults with learning difficulties or physical disabilities and for those recovering from mental illnesses. All independently run Homes are inspected and registered; local authority Homes are only inspected. The unit also *registers* small private homes (up to three residents) with a 'light touch' – which means that the sole criterion is the fitness of the Home owner to take in older people. Inspection is not compulsory, but many authorities do in fact visit small Homes and give advice.

Each independent or voluntary Home is registered for a particular category, which may be:

- general elderly people
- elderly people with confusion
- elderly people with a physical disability.

The inspection and registration unit sets out the standards of care that Homes are required to offer in the provision of short- or long-term accommodation, board and personal care. Personal care includes not only help with bodily functions but also support to enable an individual to live with dignity. Homes are inspected for:

- the fitness of the owner or manager
- the standards of the premises and facilities.

Owners who want to change to caring for a different elderly client group – typically people who are more highly dependent – will normally be inspected for the new group and their registration will be changed. They can also apply for a case-by-case exemption; for instance, if a resident becomes more dependent while living at the Home. If a proprietor wants to cater for an entirely different client group, for example younger people with learning disabilities, an entirely different set of criteria apply and the scrutiny of a person's fitness would be extremely stringent. Very few private Homes have diversified in this way, though it may be an option to consider if an owner has the relevant experience and interest. As a general rule, Home owners should always consult the inspector before making any changes that may affect staffing or the well-being of their residents.

The commissioning unit

Most local authority social services departments now have a commissioning or contracting unit. The commissioning process tends to be about overall identification of need and of the services to meet it, whilst contracting is a detailed process of developing the contract itself. The operation may vary from authority to authority. The commissioning unit may also be involved in drawing up the Community Care Plan (see p 11) which every authority is legally obliged to have. But although they have an overview of what is going on in their locality, the unit is not necessarily in touch with the details of the care needed district by district within their authority.

Assessment and care management

Care assessment and management teams are based in local districts within the larger local authority. Care management teams are employed by SSDs. They may visit older people in their own homes or they may be responsible for other members of staff who will carry out such visits to assess people's needs and level of care required. They are likely to liaise with specialist health consultants as well as social workers. The job of the team is to plan for care and acquire the services, either from the local authority social services or by purchasing services from the independent sector – including residential and nursing Homes. (For definitions of these terms, see the Glossary at the end of this book). The care manager is also responsible for monitoring individual care plans.

Looking ahead, one of the intentions of the 1990 Act was to separate purchasers and providers, so more care services will be provided by the independent sector. This is a developing area and still uncertain but, as 85 per cent of the Special Transitional Grant (STG) has to be spent in the independent sector, there has been money available for care management. This of course is not new money; it is 'recycled' from the DSS, and the STG will come to an end in 1996.

NOTE In some areas there is a new initiative, called Locality Planning, which involves the commissioning unit, care managers, providers, users and carers. The locality planning team will be responsible for assessing what is available in small areas of the authority and what will be needed. (It may eventually be as important for a Home owner to know what they are planning as what is being planned in the Community Care Plan as a whole.

Funding

One of the most important changes created by the 1990 Act has been in the way state funding is available for residents in private or voluntary

Homes. Under the Income Support system of funding, private Home owners were able to budget with reasonable certainty, knowing that their residents' fees would be paid either completely privately or that Income Support money (up to a nationally set level) would be available if an individual were eligible to receive it. This state financial support did not depend on any assessment of care need and it was given to about 30 per cent of residents in independent residential Homes through Income Support.

Some older people are still able to claim up to £198 a week from Income Support and other sources. Since April 1993, however, the state-funded cost of care for *new* residents, which would have been provided through Income Support, is made through the person's local authority, which has the duty to allocate its funds in the most appropriate way. In the past, approximately 74 per cent of residential places were funded by the public or voluntary sector (*Age File '93*, Table 6.1, Anchor Housing Trust). It is almost certain that in future this figure will drop by 20–30 per cent, though there will be regional variations.

In the future, it may be that the shortfall will be made up when older people who own their own houses – increasingly living alone – are no longer able to manage without help and decide to sell up and move into a residential Home. At the moment this is an unknown quantity. Houses are difficult to sell, and the sale of a house may still not produce sufficient income to cover all the costs. It will be necessary to use capital to cover residential fees, so an important issue for older people must be whether they have enough to cover, say, three to five years in residential care. Other options are insurance policies specifically designed to cover residential Homes, rather as current schemes cover independent school fees and pensions.

It is clearly in the owner's interest that a current or potential resident has the best possible independent financial advice. There are now a number of agencies that offer specialist advice. If you put potential clients in touch with a financial adviser, make sure that they are reputable and registered members of FIMBRA, the insurance regulatory body.

A good financial agent will look into every person's case individually. Factors to be taken into account include age and life expectancy, the level of care required, capital available through savings and/or sale of the individual's home, entitlement to state benefits and the involvement of the local authority's social services department. One such agency offers a free service which includes the following:

- Safe plans to meet the rising cost of care fees
- Advice on entitlement to DSS/local authority financial support
- Guidance on legal implications and tax matters
- Continuing free advisory service throughout care
- Advice on preserving a resident's ability to leave an inheritance.

KEY POINTS

- A person in need of care has to apply or is referred to their local SSD for an assessment, which determines both the level of care and the level of financial support for which the person is eligible.

- If a person is recommended for residential care, there may be a shortfall in the level of funding given and what the Home actually charges.

- The allowance paid varies in different parts of the country, perhaps by as much as £50 a week. If a Home has residents funded by different authorities, the owner may be able to negotiate a higher rate from an authority that pays less than the average.

- The Home owner may also have to negotiate with the resident's family to make up any shortfall in the allowances offered and the real cost of care.

- Independent specialist financial advice is available to help residents plan their future. It is in your interest to help them obtain it.

Provision of care

Care in a person's own home

One of the tenets of the 1990 Community Care Act is that, where possible, care for individuals assessed as being in need should take place in their own home if they so wish, or in conditions as similar to that as can be arranged. As a result, people assessed by the local authority as needing residential or nursing care may well be more dependent than before 1990. This represents a fundamental change. The community care reforms have also created a shift from a service-led 'take it or leave it' attitude, towards providing a service that is led by need.

Team manager 'When I started in care for elderly people, most offices sent out the least qualified junior to fill out an application for a Part III Home. That was it – you either got a bit of help at home, say two hours a week, or you were admitted to a residential Home. Now we have very highly skilled, highly qualified care managers who will go to the ends of the earth to avoid admitting people to residential care – if they want to stay at home. In this authority we can now offer seven days a week personal care, three to four visits a day and night visiting in many areas. Time and again the positive choice is to stay at home.'

It appears that the intention of the 1994 Community Care Act is that the vast majority of older people receive care where they want it – at home. A figure of 4 per cent has commonly been given for those living in institutional care of one sort or another. Even this low figure may be falling. It is an over-statement to say that the non-specialist residential Home is a thing of the past, but there are certainly people who believe that this is the case – an idea that would have been unthinkable even four years ago.

In the meantime, the responsibility of care is on the increase for all carers who look after an elderly friend or relative at home. These carers are organising themselves nationally and locally to obtain support. They are in the market for a great number of services: respite care, practical daily help, advice and also training for the demanding role they have undertaken.

Residential care

There is still a need for residential care, and here too the position has changed. The number of people aged 85+ is increasing. There are now more residential places in the independent sector than in the public sector, and in some areas demand has fallen below supply. However, in others, especially in the larger cities, there is still a shortage of appropriate residential care.

It is possible that in future more better-off older people than at present will choose to move into some kind of sheltered accommodation, and then if necessary into an associated residential or nursing Home. This is certainly a trend in the United States. In the United Kingdom, some voluntary organisations do offer these services on one site. However, most voluntary organisations prefer to help older people to 'age in place' – that is, not have to move round on a sort of conveyor belt of care.

Facilities in Homes

Although basic standards have had to be met, the facilities offered by residential Homes have varied greatly. Some provide a range of activities for their residents and look outwards, encouraging them to take part in community life. Others, often those with more frail residents, have had to concentrate on essential care. Some are in a country house setting and others are in the suburbs where it is not so easy to go for a walk or pop down to the shops. The philosophy of care in such Homes has often been inward looking and they may have been unaware of the debate on care that has taken place within their local council or how it affects them.

Assessment of need

All local authorities have to assess the financial and care needs of an older person who appears to be in need of services that they may arrange or provide. This will include both residential and nursing Home care. There are no national standards as to who will actually carry out the assessment, and, depending on an individual's needs, it may involve input from several professionals such as social worker, district nurse, occupational therapist and GP. Each authority has its own criteria to determine who is eligible for which service. The local authority sets out the bands of residential care that it applies, and the health authority is responsible for the bands of nursing care. Each band attracts a different level of allowance, Band 1 being the lowest.

Typical local authority banding for residential care

Band 1 A person in need of some support, but who may be relatively active and mobile.

Band 2 A person who needs the help of one care assistant for simple activities such as dressing or walking, getting out of a chair, or who may be mildly incontinent.

Band 3 A person with a high degree of incontinence, who needs two care assistants for tasks such as bathing or helping them get out of bed.

Typical health authority banding for nursing home care

Band 1 A patient in need of general nursing care, including washing, the administering of medicines etc, but who may be able to do some things for themselves.

Band 2 A patient who has a greater need for general nursing care.

NOTE A new concept of care is under discussion in a joint initiative between some health and local authorities. This will be for patients who have been identified as having specialist health care needs that are over and above general nursing care. These may include specialist medical care, specialist nursing care, psychiatric care, specialist occupational therapy and/or specialist equipment, and so on.

KEY POINTS

- There are no statutory national guidelines as to how people are assessed for care, either in terms of what care they need or the level of their allowance.

- The situation is changing rapidly. Both health authorities and local authorities say that there is likely to be more co-operation between them in deciding responsibilities for long-term health care.

- Owners of care Homes need to make sure that they know what their own authorities are doing about this.

THE ECONOMIC AND SOCIAL SCENE

The housing market

The current state of the housing market means that Home owners no longer have the security of knowing that their properties are increasing in value ahead of inflation; indeed they may have 'negative equity'. During the late 1980s and early 1990s there was what was known as a 'care gap'. For example, while the maximum amount of money paid by the Department of Social Security (DSS) for someone in a Home could be £194, the cost of care to the proprietor may have been actually £240–£300 (1994 figures). But as long as property prices were rising at around 15–20 per cent a year, bank managers were happy and owners had a financial cushion to fall back on.

Now the 'care gap' has been transferred from the DSS to the local authorities, who may not only be paying less than the full cost of care but are also, as a matter of policy and necessity, often decreasing the number of residential places they buy for older people in need of care. All Homes that traditionally relied on some of their income from the public sector are now competing in a shrinking market. More beds in large modified houses are standing empty.

A changing social climate

At the same time, the level of expectation from the consumers of care is rising and some Homes in the public and independent sectors are now considered to be inadequate. Housing associations have been in the vanguard in reassessing their policies both in provision of housing and in quality of care.

> 'The market place has changed during the last five years and will continue at an accelerating pace for the foreseeable future. Care in the Community, older people's rising expectations, reducing grant levels and the subsequent decrease in the development of new properties and services, are all contributing factors to the need for the Group to reconsider the manner in which it relates to its customers and end users.' *Anchor News*, December 1993.

It is worth considering this reference to older people's rising expectations in more detail because – unlike some social changes – it has not received much comment. But many people in their 60s and 70s have had a higher standard of living and a better quality of life than their own parents or even people of one generation before them. Paid holidays abroad, centrally heated housing, indoor bathrooms, modern kitchens, washing machines, videos, telephones, private sleeping accommodation have become a routine part of life for many people where once they might have been luxuries. A person who has been accustomed to privacy will find it hard to adjust to sharing a room with a stranger, walking down a corridor in the middle of the night to a toilet or even not being able to get a cup of tea until someone brings it.

Where local authorities are closing residential Homes because they are more like institutions than homes, or because they cannot afford to bring them up to registration standards, the independent sector fails to take note at its peril.

Inspector   'It's often a matter of different generations. Ten years ago there were a lot of ex-servicemen in our Homes who didn't mind doubling up and sharing a room. Today it's not acceptable and many local authority Homes have beds blocked in a double room because it's simply not suitable to put a second person in there. This is even more the case when people going into a Home are likely to be incontinent or have mobility problems and they need more space.'

The market leaders in the voluntary and private sectors are continually reviewing their policies and provision. In some cases they have modernised a block of studio flats and knocked three flats into two, to provide high-quality sheltered housing. Their units all have en-suite facilities and always with more space than required by registration.

What, then, are the major expectations today? They are likely to include:

- single rooms
- en-suite washing and toilet facilities
- a specially designed garden with plant beds at sitting level
- separate lounges for smokers and for non-smokers
- lifts for rooms above ground floor level.

Another plus would be a bar where residents could have a drink (some Homes even have a regular Happy Hour).

A Home owner may be caught between two sets of circumstances, both equally threatening to his or her business. On the one hand, fewer people are being funded to come into residential accommodation, and, on the other, those who do come into a Home, want more than may be offered, though without necessarily being able to pay much more.

What this means for home owners

The breakdown of established social patterns is part of a wider dilemma that many other groups in the workforce have had to face. Most school leavers know that they have to develop transferable skills; indeed the NVQs that Home owners should be helping their own staff to achieve are based on this premise. New jobs are created, but may be part-time; bankers, nurses, teachers, civil servants are finding that what seemed a job for life may only be a job for a short-term contract. Farmers are turning to bed and breakfast, decorators are retraining as driving instructors. For a Home owner considering diversification this means that help and advice should be available from people and organisations who have faced change themselves.

Obviously you will need to do a great deal of thinking and planning and consultation before coming to any decision about change or diversification, but knowing whom to talk to and what questions to ask is vital.

There is no single pattern of care over the whole country, although there are trends. It is important that Home owners keep in touch with what is going on locally and become politically aware. In the next chapter are some questions you may find it helpful to think about and put to the relevant person or organisation.

KEY POINTS

- Even if a Home has residents funded by the local authority, it is possible that there is a 'care gap' between what the authority pays and the true cost of care to the Home owner.

- There may be a developing market for high quality and/or specialist residential places in the future, but it is an uncertain quantity at the moment.

- The expectations of older people entering a Home and of their relatives are higher than they were in the 1970s and 1980s.

- Single rooms are likely to be the norm unless residents ask to share.

- It is important for all Home owners to consider their future and their options *now*.

- Most older people will be cared for in their own home as a first choice.

- Local authorities will usually arrange for an older person to go into residential care only if they are frail, disabled, confused or mentally ill and where care at home proves too difficult to provide or too expensive.

- Residents with preserved rights will continue to be funded by the DSS at well below the actual cost of care in some areas.

OPPORTUNITIES FOR CHANGE

Every organisation needs to look regularly at its marketing strategy and, even if it is non-profit making, make sure that it is reaching the widest client group for its services. This is as important for the voluntary sector as for private Home owners. The voluntary sector may also need to diversify if it is to survive. It is worth breaking this down into two areas – the best use of the buildings and premises, and the best uses of the skills and resources of the staff.

Many Homes were adapted for their present use in the 1970s and early 1980s. They may not now provide the kind of facilities that older people are increasingly beginning to expect or that meet current guidelines. You may attract more business if you upgrade what you offer.

Finding new markets

The most obvious change of direction, as mentioned earlier, is to take on a *more dependent clientele*, those who are frail, confused or in need of special care. This will need further registration and inspection (see p 13).

It is unlikely that you would be eligible to register a Home for *adults with learning difficulties, drug dependency* or *mental health problems* or for *children in need of care* without suitable buildings and highly qualified staff to run it, but it is an option if you can fulfil the different criteria. You would have fewer clients but a higher income per client because you would be providing very specialist, and possibly intensive, care.

You may decide to apply for *dual registration* – that is, to operate as both a residential and a nursing Home. At the moment this means being inspected by both the local authority and the health authority and employing qualified nurses. However, there is an overlap of care and the difference between both types of Home is increasingly considered to be a grey area. As mentioned earlier, some experts believe that in five years' time there will be only one registration authority for both – and one category, that of care Home.

Related to nursing, but in a very specialised way, is *hospice care*. There is a great need for sensitive care of people with terminal illness, and it may be that you could consider this if you have a nursing background and wish to move out of straight residential care (see p 67). You would need to be very sure of your funding, because the SSD does not pay for patients in hospices and the Department of Health (DoH) has limited resources.

On the other hand, you may decide to look into the provision of a type of *sheltered housing* and, if the premises are suitable, adapt sets of rooms to provide small flats, a communal dining room and lounge and a resident warden (see p 65).

Respite care for people who live in their own homes would involve neither further inspection nor registration but simply letting people know that you offer it (see p 51). However, you should consult with your registration officer, as well as with your residents and staff, about the implications.

Further alternatives

All these suggestions have implied that you will operate primarily as a residential Home or building for long-stay residents. However, you may decide to explore diversification in a wider sense to make full use of your own skills or interests and those of your staff.

Day care may be a possibility if you have reception room space. A few day visitors may be easily assimilated into your present accommodation, but it may be more appropriate to set aside rooms especially for people looking for day care full-time or for a few hours a week (see pp 53–55 for discussion of day care provision).

Domiciliary care involves taking personal care into people's own homes – perhaps on an emergency basis, perhaps regularly through contracts with individuals or the local social services (see pp 59–61).

There are other special services such as laundry, gardening and meals which may be very valuable for older people in your neighbourhood. They can take up spare capacity, make good care sense and may be a first step into branching out further. If your Home has facilities for helping residents into and out of the bath, perhaps you could offer these to people living in their own homes. These services also act as an advertisement for the Home even if they do not run at a profit (see p 60), and may in the end lead to people becoming permanent residents.

Closing down

This is not an option that you may anticipate now, but it may turn out to be the most realistic when you have examined the market, done your research and talked to your bank manager and local authority. Estimates at this time are that between 30 and 50 per cent of residential Homes may have to cease trading within the next four or five years. Some local authorities have virtually run out of money for new placements. Some Homes will diversify, others will find new markets. You may be able to trade down – take on smaller premises – or you may decide that the most sensible way to go forward is to come to a halt. Closure, like expansion, needs careful planning for yourself and for your residents. It is better – both for you and for your residents – to do it as a conscious decision early rather than lose everything because it is forced upon you. For details about planning to close down, see Appendix 1 (p 116).

KEY POINTS

- Local and national politics can affect your business. Know what goes on.
- Talk to and consult as many people as possible in the private and public sectors.
- It is better to anticipate change than wait till it is forced upon you.
- Make sure that you offer what the purchasers want.
- Older people today expect better standards all round than they did ten years ago.
- In many areas the residential sector is contracting in size. There is a limit to what you can do.
- Homes that offer a quality service at a competitive cost are the ones most likely to survive.

2 Taking Stock

This chapter is designed to help you take a realistic view of your business and the implications for change at a management and personal level. It is very easy to focus entirely on bricks and mortar, because these represent such a large investment. Home owners who went into business in the 1980s have probably seen the value of their investment go down and the gap between income and expenditure go up.

- Large loans and an overdraft are set against a sum that is higher than the buildings are now actually worth – negative equity.

- Beds are empty in Homes that aim for a high standard of care as well as those that offer a more basic level.

But you have invested more than cash, you have invested perhaps five or ten or twenty years of your life in skills and experience. Of course, some Home owners have gone into their business solely for profit – as in any business – but very many have also wanted to contribute to the quality of care for older people at the end of their lives. So this may be the moment to examine again how you can use that experience in a way that fulfils your goals and also provides the rewards of hard work – that is to say, a healthy bank balance.

Human resources are more than you and your family. They also include the people you work with, your staff and your clients – the residents, their families and the care managers in the local authority. It is they who contribute to the goodwill that is part of any business. In some countries such as Japan they are considered to be a major part of the company – more so than shareholders, who are not involved in the day-to-day decisions. So it is important to look not only at your own interests and skills but also at those of the people around you. This chapter will help you take stock of all aspects of your establishment and prepare a set of working documents with which you can reach informed decisions to prepare a business plan. They include:

- Where your business or establishment has reached
- Financial assets and liabilities
- Your current care provision
- Your current clients or customers

NOTE The term 'you' is used when making suggestions in the section below. However, you may prefer at this stage to set up a 'taking stock' group or committee if you have the resources. This will save you energy, bring in people with different viewpoints, and may prove cost effective in the long run.

WHERE ARE YOU NOW? – AN OVERVIEW

In 1994 one of the 'gurus' of the business world, Charles Handy, published a book called *The Empty Raincoat*. In it he describes the natural rise-and-fall pattern of organisations, or empires, or a person's life. He demonstrates this by a visual image, the Sigmoid Curve (or 'developmental curve'), which is like a double S or sine wave.

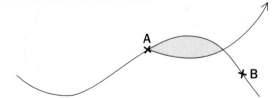

Figure 1: Sigmoid Curve

Handy suggests that an organisation has its ups and downs in terms of development and profit until it starts on a final downward curve. At that point it has to come to an end in closure or bankruptcy. To keep going you have to start a new curve, and the best moment for that is just before the final crest, at point A. The time each organisation takes to reach point A is different – an empire may take 150 years to decline and fall, a business can go downhill in ten years. In our own lives there may be several different curves. If the best moment to move is before the first curve fades, for a time two curves will be running together.

A person or business at point A has to go through the difficult and challenging process of asking questions, looking at goals, seeing where the new curve will take them. The problem is that many of us looking back, if we are honest, can see that we often made changes a bit late, on the downward slope at point B, rather than just before the crest of the wave.

Questions to consider

Can you see this kind of pattern in your own life or business?

Try to assess honestly where your business is on its Sigmoid Curve. Is it:

- Still on the upward slope at point A or earlier?
- On the crest of the wave?
- On the way down, at point B?

Handy suggests that organisations near point A on the curve will need to change their present strategies within two or three years. Look carefully at where you have placed yourself. Try to think through the implications, both for yourself and for the business.

According to this theory, when is the best time for your business to move to the second curve?

- Within the next year?
- Within the next three years?
- Not in the foreseeable future?

Your own position

Take another look at the Sigmoid Curve and relate it to your own life.

Questions to consider

On a personal level:

- Are you ready to move on to a different curve?
- Are you a long way before point A?
- Do you have the energy and commitment to make changes?

- Do you as a person welcome change, or do you prefer to do the same thing for a long time?
- Do you have the necessary leadership and management skills?
- Do you have proper back-up?
- Can you cope under extra stress?

These are just a few questions you should ask yourself. There are a number of self-assessment books which you may find helpful to look through (see Further Reading). Or you may prefer to take professional advice from a business or management consultant. Your local Training and Enterprise Council (TEC) should be able to put you in touch with someone suitable.

The previous section should have helped you to assess your personal position. The rest of this chapter is designed to help you take stock of the Home itself – how it is set up and financed, how it is administered and how it fits in with the wider community. But to start with, what are the underlying principles of care that you offer? Do they enable you to develop good corporate policy that will improve the quality of care that you offer so that there will be increased demand for your services?

THE PHILOSOPHY OF THE HOME

Many Homes in the independent and public sectors have a philosophy of care that they have drawn up over perhaps two or three years, after consulting everyone who may be affected – and this includes care or nursing staff as well as management. Extracts from the philosophy of care of Anchor Housing Trust are given below.

OUR PHILOSOPHY

1   In caring for each elderly person, we will keep a clear focus on the needs and wishes of each resident and will follow these fundamental principles:

   a   respect for each individual and his/her personal background/culture;

   b   enabling residents to continue their chosen lifestyle;

   c   offering individual residents opportunities for new friendships and experience within the community life;

d listening and responding to the views and comments of residents, relatives and friends;

e providing personal care that is discreet, sensitive and appropriate to the needs of each individual;

f giving residents a real say in the running of the establishment.

2 Each member of staff will understand and share these principles and values, and we will only recruit staff who can demonstrate their commitment to providing excellent care.

3 All care practices will be based on these principles and we will constantly seek to improve them.

4 All staff will be listened to and supported by their manager. We are committed to the following:

a free and open communication;

b training and education enabling our principles and necessary caring skills to be put into practice;

c all levels of staff contributing to decision-making;

d building teams that give support and encouragement to everyone;

e recognising success;

f assisting all of us to gain job satisfaction;

g providing opportunities for personal and career development.

Questions to consider

- Does your Home have a written mission or philosophy?
- Do the residents as well as the staff have a copy?
- Are you satisfied that it is understood and carried out in practice?

LOOKING AT FINANCE

This is a very necessary part of taking stock. It means making a realistic and detailed account of your exact financial position. If you are not a trained accountant, you should involve a professional accountant at this stage to draw up a list of all your assets and liabilities or to check your figures. The figures should include the following.

Capital investment

- The current value of the property
- Bank or other loans, including working capital
- Overdrafts and interest payments
- Equipment etc.

You will probably have these headings to hand in your yearly accounts. However, many of the figures will be nominal. What is needed here is not the book value of your investment, but what it is actually worth on the open market. In other words, can you continue to operate, given your current financial position, or are you running up larger and larger overdrafts while your asset values are declining?

Running the business

This involves looking in detail at exactly where the money goes. Again, you will probably have figures from your accounts, but your budget may cover very broad areas. A good bookkeeper will be your best ally here to check out the different areas of your establishment. This will provide you with a basis to see if you can make the business more efficient without lowering the quality of care. Aim to have a working document that will show you exactly what every area costs – where the money goes.

Break down each area into as much detail as you can. What are your costs each week/month on full-time and on part-time staff; what are your total National Insurance costs?

Questions to consider

- Management fees
- Staff
- Food
- Repairs and renewals
- Linen and laundry
- General upkeep
- Garden
- Other

Steps to take

When you have all the figures, collate them into a document that is useful for yourself, not for a financier or banker. They can be turned into the shape that accountants like when or if you make a formal business plan based on your findings.

YOUR CURRENT PROVISION

Carry out a similar exercise about your actual provision in the areas of accommodation, board and personal care.

Accommodation

The first step is to make a precise analysis of the accommodation you offer. No doubt you have one. Is it up to date?

Questions to consider

- Number of single rooms
- Number of double or multi-occupancy rooms
- Number of rooms with en-suite facilities
- Maximum size of rooms required for registration
- Number of public rooms
  What they are used for
  What their size is
  Potential for development
- Sets of rooms that could be knocked through to provide en-suite bathrooms or kitchenettes
- The cost feasibility of relocating residents while improvements are made
- State of repair and decoration
  In good repair
  In need of a coat of paint or new wallpaper
  In need of stripping down and refurbishment to bring it up to modern standards

Upgrading facilities

While you are considering this, also examine the general quality of the care you offer. Could or should that be upgraded as well?

Questions to consider

- What about somewhere to make a cup of tea? Is it within easy access for those who would like to use this?
- Things that could be done without much expense.
- Upgrading that would be possible but expensive.

Steps to take

- Visit some other Homes that may have been refurbished or adapted for care use. Note what they offer that is different, and perhaps better, from that in your Home.
- Talk to your own residents, their relatives or representatives.
- Discuss it with your care staff. They may have contacts with other carers.
- Make preliminary inquiries about how much it might cost, perhaps converting a few rooms at a time.
- Look into the possibilities of making up 'unitised' sets of rooms, which are often more suitable for mentally infirm residents.

Board and personal care

These are the basic requirements that all residential Homes contract to provide for the people to whom they offer a home. The quality of what you offer will make the difference between its being a real home or just somewhere to pass the rest of their days. What is the nature and quality of the care that you provide? Does your Home belong to a professional trade association that is able to give you wider support?

Questions to consider
Meals

- Do you offer meals in residents' own rooms or only in the dining room?
- Is there provision for snacks in rooms?
- Are meal times flexible?

Food

- Do you check with residents what they would actually like to eat?
- Are you up to date about appropriate food for older people?
- Do you offer plenty of fresh fruit, vegetables etc?
- How much of the food would be called 'home made'?
- Has your cook been on a refresher course?
- Do you offer a good choice of menu or does it tend to be a long-term weekly list without much variation?
- Do you offer special diets for religious or personal reasons, as well as for medical ones?

The care plan

- Does every resident have a personal care plan (sometimes called a service personal provision plan) with which they have been personally involved and approved?
- Is it kept up to date?
- Are relatives involved in decision-making, as well as medical and nursing consultants?
- Do you have a clear policy on managing risks, which you have discussed with individual residents as well as relatives, where appropriate?

Routine care

- Are all members of staff trained to help settle in new arrivals?
- Does each resident have one personal or key worker whom they can refer to?
- Do you have a system whereby day and night workers can let others know if a resident needs extra care or attention?

Special care

- Does every person who needs it have access to personal therapies, both for the body and for the mind?
- Do you have regular groups (eg reminiscence or physiotherapy), if appropriate?
- Do you have enough equipment for mobility, lifting, etc? List what you have.

- When did you last look into new aids for mobility?
- Does the Home have a policy about the use of medicines?

Activities

- How do residents pass their time? Just sitting or watching television or do you provide:
  a library of large print books
  music tapes or records
  regular games or entertainment sessions
  visiting volunteers for special occasions
  regular outings to cinema, theatre or the countryside
  anything extra
- Is there good access to grounds and places for people to sit?
- Are there places where people can go for privacy?

Profile of the staff

This profile should include not only the numbers of staff but also the personal qualities of the care, domestic and administrative staff who work with you. It is helpful to take such an overview of their attitudes and abilities because you may have engaged them on an ad hoc basis and there may be skills or personal qualities that are not covered. For instance, you may not have needed to employ anyone used to leading a reminiscence group or able to bath someone who is severely disabled. If you decide to offer care for older people with a higher degree of frailty, you will need care assistants with these skills or experience.

Questions to consider

- How many full-time and part-time staff do you employ?
- What are their special skills?
- How long have they been with you?
- What is the level of support and training available to staff? Is there on-going training?
- Do you find it easy to introduce new staff (ie are they made welcome by the others)?
- Do you encourage them to work as a team?

- Do they take responsibility?
- Do they know when to refer to a manager if there is a problem?
- How many could you keep on and retrain if you diversify?
- Which members of staff might find it hard to work with a different client group?
- Do some have special skills or interests that you could develop?

Profile of the residents

Questions to consider

- Number of residents currently in the Home.
- Maximum numbers possible for your current and a different client group.
- Degree of frailty:
  take an interest in what goes on;
  able to get about on their own;
  mentally frail;
  physically frail.
- Funded from:
  Income Support (pre April 1993);
  local authority contract;
  private income.
- People with personal/emotional support from:
  relatives or friends;
  an advocate;
  a voluntary group or agency.
- Numbers from similar social class or background:
  higher income;
  lower income;
  rural;
  urban.

WHAT IS GOING ON IN YOUR LOCAL AUTHORITY?

An important part of taking stock is making sure you know just what is going on in your local area. Chapter 1 suggested a number of ways in which you can get to know what is going on in your area, and stressed the importance of personal contacts. It would be helpful at this stage to put together the information you have found out, and to set up personal contacts. When considering your local authority, remember to include not only people from the social services department but also the politicians who employ them. Many local councillors have areas of special interest – they are certainly used to being lobbied – and the care of older people in the community has a higher profile than a few years ago. Have you asked any of your local councillors – perhaps the mayor – to come and have tea in the Home? A list of people or departments you should talk to is set out below, together with some questions that you may wish to ask, including finding out about your local Community Care Plan.

The first place to seek advice is the from the social services department of your local authority, and here there will be the units mentioned in Chapter 1.

- The *inspection and registration unit*, which you will have already dealt with in registering your Home.

- The new *commissioning* or *contracting unit* which is responsible for contracting various care services from the independent sector.

- The *care manager*, responsible for arranging the provision of care services in the area, and who may be able to offer you individual-type contracts.

All these units should be able to give you an overview of the circumstances in your particular area: are they over- or under-subscribed with residential places, what respite or domiciliary services are needed, what gaps are there in provision and what standards do they expect before contracting your places or services? It is vital that you take these factors into consideration. The most important questions are: what services are they planning to purchase and what arrangements are they going to make to inform the independent sector of their tendering arrangements.

The Community Care Plan

As mentioned in Chapter 1, each local authority must draw up a plan which is published after consultation with local carers, users, purchasers and providers. It is regularly updated and modified. This is the blueprint for all future care in your area, so it is essential reading for every Home owner before talking to anyone. Have you or your representative been consulted about your local Community Care Plan? Have you even seen it?

Question to ask
- Where can I see a copy?

The Government has set aside funds, the Special Transitional Grant (STG), to cover care for older people in need either of residential care or of services in their own home. The grant reflects the shift in funding residential and nursing Home care from the DSS to local authorities. However, the STG ends in 1996 and it is not clear what will happen to funding after then.

Question to ask
- What is happening to that money in our area?

Although social workers have tended in the past to be suspicious of privately run Homes, this attitude is changing. You can help this process by showing that you are open to ideas and are willing to listen to what they say. If you run a Home that values the dignity of the residents and is doing a good job, make sure that the local authority know about it, and persevere in asking care managers to come round to see what you do – and to talk to you.

Question to ask
- Why don't you come and see what we're doing?

Some local authorities are closing down their own Homes. This may lead to opportunities for private Homes in those areas.

Questions to ask
- What are the plans for these local authority Homes if there are closures, and where will the residents be going?
- Where will new residents be going?

The commissioning unit should have an overview of demographic trends, the numbers of people needing care and the sort of care required – whether residential or domiciliary. Use their expertise.

Questions to ask

- How do you see the role of the independent sector in providing care in the community?
- Where are the gaps?
- How many places will you buy next year in my area?
- Do you give block contracts for services such as respite care, laundry or meals?

If you are thinking about admitting residents who have a higher degree of dependency, you may need to take on more staff with specialist skills and to make alterations to the buildings – which may be costly. The inspection and registration unit has experience of both and should give you preliminary advice.

Questions to ask

- What are the changes I need to make to cater for a higher level of disability or frailty?
- Is there another Home owner, perhaps not in my immediate neighbourhood, whom you could put me in touch with?
- Is there a local Association I could join for advice and support?

Older people and their carers

The needs of these groups are not of course the same, but they are linked. A carer may need a break from the daily and repetitive tasks involved in looking after one person full-time, the older person may long for a break from the carer and a change of diet and conversation. A spell of respite care in your Home, which can be anything from a few hours a week to a few weeks, may suit both. It can also be at night rather than during the day. There should be representatives of both groups locally, such as your branch of Age Concern, a Relatives Association or a group of carers such as the Carers National Association and the Carers Forum, whom you should talk to about their particular needs.

NOTE   It may not be practicable for you to offer short-term care to someone who is confused. There are often problems with the transition from their own home to a residential Home. Respite care in this case would provide two sets of problems, on arrival and on departure. In such cases, the best approach may be to suggest that relatives bring a person with confusion to the Home for day care, so that they can get used to the Home gradually.

Some questions to ask

- What is the normal length of respite care you require?

- How can I, as a manager, make respite care special? Is it food, companionship, different facilities from home?

- Are there any facilities that we can offer carers who are at work (eg special transport)?

- What sort of price would you be prepared to pay if we offered domiciliary care?

- Would other help such as laundry and meals be of interest or use to carers?

The health care team

Doctors and nurses are an important part of health care, and increasingly work from health centres that provide a range of care services for all ages. They see people at all stages in their lives, and they probably understand not just physical disabilities but also their emotions – hopes and fears and desires. Some health workers are in and out of residential Homes regularly to visit their patients. Others may not be aware of what a Home has to offer.

Questions to ask

- Have you heard of our Home?

- Are you a fund-holding practice? If so, do you purchase any nursing or other care?

- Would you recommend ancillary services, such as help with the house or garden, if we were to offer it?

RELATIONSHIP WITH THE COMMUNITY

Undoubtedly there will be many more questions you will think of putting, and other people to contact, among them other businesses in your area. Some of these are listed below.

- religious organisations
- voluntary agencies
- relatives' groups
- local carers
- local groups such as the Women's Institute
- local chamber of commerce
- small business group

ADMINISTRATIVE SYSTEMS

A good many Homes that were set up in the 1980s are still behind in the use of modern technology. But for a small business, as well as a large one, a modern computer and suitable software packages are essential tools to save time and build efficiency. What do you have?

Hardware

A modern IBM-compatible or Apple computer with at least 170Mb of memory should meet your needs.

Software

There is a wide range of specialist packages for residential Homes that will make it extremely quick for you to develop your systems and update your records.[1]

---

[1] Remember that, under the 1990 Data Protection Act, you are obliged to show their computerised record to any member of staff or resident who asks to see them.

- rotas and other forms
- records of residents
- records of staff
- contract management
- accounts

This is discussed in Chapter 7.

YOUR MANAGEMENT STYLE AND PRACTICE

It is important to see not only how you do things but also why. It cannot be stressed enough that you are entering a very competitive market. SSDs will go for what they term 'preferred suppliers' – providers whom they believe consistently provide quality care. Establishments that deliver quality will attract more clients and more cash per case if that is appropriate. In some local authorities this means that there may be a premium for Homes with care staff who have NVQs or SNVQs, residents committees etc.

Is your management style up to date? How does it fit into some of the current ideas about the best way to run a business organisation? Charles Handy (of the Sigmoid Curve), Tom Peters and other management consultants have devoted a lot of time researching the ways that successful – and not so successful – companies operate. Some of the new thinking is particularly helpful when a business is developing or changing. An outline is given below, with some questions they may raise for your own business practice.

Total quality management

This means that the process of management is continually being reassessed and redefined. It is a concept developed particularly by Japanese companies, and has led to practices such as quality circles and team briefing (see the Glossary). It means that, through good management, the quality of the service (or of the goods) is continually being appraised and raised.

Questions to consider

- Has the management style changed since you set up the business?
- How often do you:
  hold regular staff meetings?
  ask for suggestions to improve working methods?
  make changes as a result of a your own research or a suggestion?
  give regular training for all staff, not only for new members?
  tell the staff what is going on – the problems as well as the positive things?
- Can you involve the staff more in the day-to-day running of the Home?
- Have you organised regular staff support and supervision?

Benchmarking

This means that a business looks carefully at companies in the same as well as in different sectors in order find the best way of doing something – a good-practice guide.

Questions to consider

- How much contact do you have with other Homes in your area?
- Do you exchange ideas?
- Have you contacted a local chamber of commerce or small business group?
- Have you talked to your local Training and Enterprise Council (TEC)?

Core operation

This means identifying very carefully exactly what the core of a business is, concentrating on that and letting go or contracting out goods or services that are outside the core.

Core operation is at the heart of the current political philosophy of the government, in theory if not always in practice. For example, local councils are elected to make sure that, among other things, the streets are clean and rubbish is collected regularly. Traditionally, local authorities employed their own refuse collection staff. But is collecting rubbish a core part of government? Most councils now put out refuse collection to contract. In the same way, local authorities are encouraged to contract out their care services.

Case study

A useful example from the business world is the changing fortunes of Terence Conran, the furniture designer. He started his own shop – very exclusive designs, very expensive. He perceived a market for simple, well structured, less expensive furniture and opened a string of Habitat shops. Their business and design principles were very clear and focused.

Then in the 1980s, Conran and his board expanded into a whole business empire that included BHS and Mothercare and others in the Storehouse group, all with very different marketing and design philosophies. By the end of the decade the business was in trouble and split.

Sir Terence once more has a very elegant furniture designer shop in Kensington, Habitat has been sold to a Swedish company with a similar approach to its own design philosophy, and BHS and Mothercare are in their original place in the high street. They have all gone back to their core competences.

Back to basics

Each time a business redefines what it wants to do and is best at, there is usually some restructuring, both of systems and of staff. It means concentrating on strengths that competitors may have difficulty in imitating, and letting go or losing those that take up too much effort or are not cost-effective.

It may be that in diversifying you will need to change your core business.

Questions to consider

- How would you define the core aspects of your business? Do they include:
  an understanding of the needs of older people at a physical, emotional and spiritual level?
  the ability to create a good work environment?
  the ability to create a good homely environment?

the ability to provide care that is well thought out and respects the rights and dignity of older people?

- What are the organisational strengths of your business? Does it depend on:
  good team-work and communications?
  always getting a lead from management?
  good supervisory staff?
  well trained care assistants?
  other?

- What competences could be improved:
  interpersonal skills?
  skills in coping without supervision?
  dealing with paperwork?
  special care for people with confusion?
  special care for people who are physically disabled?
  other?

- What does my Home provide that its competitors may not? For example:
  it is well placed for good relations with the community;
  it is frequently recommended by local GPs or social workers;
  visitors and residents say it offers a friendly, caring atmosphere;
  there are pets around;
  it provides space for a number of activities.

- Do you have personal skills and contacts that make your business stand out from the others? What are they?

- Can you define the main strengths of your business?

- Are there any parts of it that you should dispose of or change?

Changing the process

This may mean a fundamental change in the way a company does business or small changes with far-reaching results. It is as important for a small as for a larger company – it is all too easy to carry on doing things the way they have always been done.

Housing association director 'I recently set up a care alert line which went directly to my office from all our Homes. It's been used four times over the last year, when care assistants have phoned up to tell me we are not meeting the target for a particular issue. They were very surprised to find themselves talking to the director, but it sent some powerful signals that we are trying to be open to suggestions and we are trying to listen.'

Changing the structure often means moving from a hierarchy to a flatter organisation, with more responsibility for everyone. The key worker system is a good example of how practice in giving care has changed over the last ten years.

Empowerment

This is often combined with changing a process. A key worker, for instance, is empowered by working with residents in a different and more personal way. It is intended to develop initiative among the staff to give them job satisfaction and to improve co-ordination of complex care tasks, which will improve the day-to-day care of your residents. The questions below are designed to highlight areas where change might benefit both your business and the level of job satisfaction of your staff.

Questions to consider

- Where does the power lie in your Home:
  with the manager in charge of a formal hierarchy?
  with the senior staff on a reasonably equal basis?
  in a strong team system that is based on key workers and a team leader?
- Do you have a key worker system?
- If the answer is 'no', have you considered it?
- If the answer is 'yes', would you agree that key workers are:
  used to working on their own?
  able to take responsibility?
  willing to contribute ideas?
  able to build up good relationships with older people?
  not always willing to refer back or consult with their team leader or management?
- What advantages would empowerment give you if you diversify the business?

- If you decide to diversify the business:
do you think that a strong hierarchy or a flatter organisation would be more suitable in your particular circumstances?
what are the reasons?
what steps, if any, would you have to take to set it up?

KEY POINTS

- It is important to recognise the current pattern of your business.

- The most successful businesses are ones that allow change and are flexible.

- The business that survives in a difficult economic climate is the one that stands out from the competition.

3 Options for change

This chapter and the next look in detail at the possibilities for developing your Home that were outlined in Chapter 1. *This chapter* also includes a survey of typical difficulties you may encounter both at a management and at a personal level. Although some of the suggestions may not be relevant to your own business, others could be helpful. Use them as a source of ideas and keep an open mind. Remember that you have not one but two major assets: your housing stock and your human resources.

WORKING WITH CHANGE

Many people find it hard to face change in their business or personal lives. It can make us afraid, irritable or depressed. We dither over simple decisions. Our minds don't seem to think clearly. In Appendix 1 there is a lot of advice on the importance of giving support if a Home is going to close down. It is just as important to find support if the Home is going to diversify.

Below are some suggestions that may help to provide this support. Unless you have enormous resources of energy and are able to cope with several things at the same time, it makes sense to consider changes with a team of people, rather than attempt to do it single-handed or in a small partnership. You may have to pay for this advice or service. In the long run, it could be money well spent. Home owners who have diversified emphasise that, however hard you may find it to let go of the reins a little, it is extremely important not to over-stretch yourself – or both the old and the new businesses will suffer.

- Set up an advisory committee or group to look at the possible options in detail.

- Appoint individual members or sub-groups to the various tasks: market research, business plan, cash-flow forecast, checking out the competition, talking to the local authority commissioning unit and the care manager.

- Draw up briefing documents for each task and get the sub-groups to amend them.

- Set a timetable for each section to report back.

- Make a deadline for the final decision and stick to it.

Once a final decision has been reached, a new steering group should be appointed to set the changes in motion.

The sections that follow are designed to give basic guidelines about what to take into account at this thinking and planning stage. They are set out under 'Questions to consider'. You could use them as a basis for a briefing document to an advisory group if you have set one up.

If you decide to explore any of the options further, the section 'Steps to take' will look at positive actions. Obviously any major steps suggested should be taken only if and when you decide to go ahead.

There are also some general points that should be considered with every option. These are outlined below.

Checklist for each option

Management and staffing

Many of the options will involve a different staffing level, and so you will need to restructure your staffing arrangements. You should look at:

- The nature of the new management structure. Do you propose to manage the whole business yourself or will you need to appoint another manager and run the business as two or more companies?

- How many new care assistants or domestic staff you will need.

- Qualifications or experience necessary for the different client groups.

- The systems you will set up to monitor quality of care.

- Administrative back-up to follow it through.

Is there demand for your chosen option?

Making sure that there is demand for the option you favour will involve detailed research and the ability to create a good marketing strategy. Are you confident that you can do this?

Relationship with the local authority

Having a good working relationship with the local authority is crucial for anyone who hopes to rely on local authority contracts with private Homes. If there is some suspicion among the care management team, you will have to work hard on personal contacts and prove that you can deliver what they want. It may be easier to work through a franchise system (described on p 61).

Are the necessary alterations too costly?

You will find this out only after you have obtained a set of estimates and worked out a proper business plan.

Diversification will require new skills

Good training is the key to getting skills in a new area. Can you obtain this locally, or through a distance learning course?

Change will put a big strain on the Home

You should not under-estimate the effort that making change will require. You should consider getting support from a recognised counsellor or therapist who is qualified in managing change. It may prove helpful for you and your staff. Any changes you may make are likely to have an impact on both residents and their families. You will need to inform and consult them from an early stage.

Upgrading your facilities

If you are considering diversification because you do not have enough residents in the Home, this may not be the best moment to talk about improving it. However, it may be the key to new markets from both the private and the public sector. If you have not changed the facilities since the early 1990s, you would be well advised to look very seriously at what you have to offer.

Housing association director 'We all have higher expectations, just as we do if we go to a hotel or bed-and-breakfast. Single bedrooms and private toilet and washing facilities are becoming an expected standard. There may be medical advantages too. We had a lady with dementia who came into one of our Homes and immediately became incontinent, which she had never been before. There were no physical reasons for this. When the care staff discussed it with her daughter they found out that she had always taught her daughter that public toilets were dirty. Now here she was in a residential Home where there were shared toilets, but it was logged deep in her brain that this was not right. So she spent her time wandering the corridors looking for her own private toilet. As soon as she was given her own facilities she stopped being incontinent.'

EXTENDING YOUR RANGE

Respite care

The first option you may like to consider is to extend the range of the residential services you offer. This is likely to be in the field of short-term care. It is often a first step towards diversifying on a larger scale and can make good use of empty rooms. However, as with other changes, you will need to talk to your residents and staff before making firm decisions.

Social care There are a number of occasions when an older person may decide to come into a Home for short period, perhaps to give their carer a break from the daily routine.

Convalescence care You may also be able to offer this to a person who is being discharged from hospital but who is not yet able to lead an active life. This could include some *nursing care*, under the direction of the district nurse, or *rehabilitation* – helping an older person to get back on their feet with specialist input from occupational or physiotherapists.

This is a market that seems to be developing, but it is not clear at present who is to pay for such services. You should make sure about policy in your area before developing your plans. Also read the note on possible new developments at the end of 'Health authority banding' on page 18 and keep in touch with your own district health authority.

The Home as part of the community

It may be possible to develop the potential of the Home by establishing it as part of the wider community. This will depend very much on where you are situated, the type of clientele you would hope to attract and who would pay for the services. There are two options here:

- To develop the Home as a social centre for older people in the neighbourhood.
- To offer flexible day and night care services.

The Home as a social centre

For this option, the possibilities vary according to the circumstances. For example, the Home could be open at certain times of the week during the day, and/or during the evening or for meals, charging a fee to those who come. Events could include:

- games and quiz sessions
- a hairdressing morning or afternoon
- exercise and occupational therapy.

If you can use the skills that your care staff already possess, the scheme should at least break even on cost. It can be enriching to the visitors and to your own residents and staff, and it will bring potential clients into the Home on an informal basis.

You will have to ensure that the residents are fully consulted, as this is first and foremost their home. The inspectorate will want to be sure that residents are not affected adversely. You will need to check out fire and health and safety regulations if you propose to bring more people into the building. This may also have implications in extending the use of the kitchen.

Questions to consider

- Look at your reception rooms to see if one of them could be used as a social centre or kind of 'club'.

- What changes or different furniture would it need?
- What about staffing? Are there relatives or local volunteer groups who would be willing to take part?
- What are the implications for fire and health and safety regulations?
- Talk to all the regular visitors to the Home, including social workers, GPs, health visitors and religious organisations.
- Consult the local care manager about whether they could make use of the new facilities.
- Consult your own residents. How would they view it – would they want to take part?

Steps to take

- Get detailed estimates of any financial outgoings.
- Prepare a budget for staff and advertising.
- Cost what you need to charge.
- Carry out a pilot study. Offer a popular event on a regular basis for a trial period such as three months. Monitor attendance, enthusiasm, ease of operation and any problems, including financial difficulties.
- Ask for regular feedback from clients and residents.
- If the venture proves a success, decide whether it is cost-effective and whether you should continue or expand to other areas.
- Assess the impact of the new venture on referrals for long-term care.

The Home as a day care centre

This is an idea that can be as simple or as structured as you want to make it. One Home with a sunny spot has built a conservatory on to the main building. It is used by six or seven day visitors, who look out on to an attractive garden. They have their lunch in the regular dining room, and sit in the other lounges if they want to have a change or to watch television. Day visitors feel at home in the house, but they have their own space and independence. Some have moved from day to respite and then long-term care, because they like the atmosphere.

In a more formal set-up, a complete set of rooms has been set aside for day care with separate dining room, lounge and washing facilities. Here there are 15 regular day visitors, with their own care staff and they do not mix with permanent residents except in the garden.

What you should consider

Day care is an option that is quite often recommended, but one that needs careful research. It can be worth while if it uses up spare capacity in the Home. However, if you need to put in extra staff or new buildings, it can become very expensive. You should check out the cost very carefully.

There are already a number of schemes in most local authorities which are run either in their own Homes or through a contract with a voluntary agency or a local group such as Age Concern. The social services team may charge as little as £2 per person per day. You may not find it cost-effective to charge less than £25 a day. You will probably need to spend money to set up a scheme and bring the premises up to specification. You will have to be able to staff it. What can you offer that is better than your competitors?

You need to be very sure of a market before going into day care in a big way. Even then, it will take a lot of day visitors to make up the loss of revenue if you are trying to fill the gap left by a shortfall in long-term residents.

NOTE Transport is a major issue in day care. Frail older people take a long time to get on and off vehicles, and may need to be settled in when they return home. This is expensive in staff time. Remember that escorts may be needed on the vehicles.

You need to determine carefully what your main considerations are in setting up a day centre. Are they:

- Marketing, as a lead into long-term care?
- Intended to provide a service that pays for itself?
- Intended to generate a substantial income?

Questions to consider

- Talk to the purchasing department of your social services team to get an assessment of day care facilities and needs in your area.
- If there is a need for day care, draw up two or three different plans and cost them separately.

- Will you need extra transport, such as a converted minibus?
- Who will pay for transport and escorts?
- Can you make sure that the rights and privacy of your long-term residents are respected?
- Look at the different levels of income the day centre could generate with different numbers of day clients; for example, 6, 10 or 15.
- What is your break-even point? Can you reach it?
- Finally, consider running a day care centre separate from the Home (eg one day a week in a church hall).

Steps to take

- Check that you have appropriate accommodation and that it will recieve the approval of the inspectorate.
- Decide what scale of day care you will be able to offer.
- Check out staffing and transport requirements.

The Home as a training centre

It is already common practice for a group of Homes to work together in training their staff. If your Home has suitable rooms, you could offer training on a regular basis to cover all aspects of care. You could provide it to care assistants in other Homes, to senior staff and managers and to independent carers who look after an older person in their own homes. The importance of such sessions is not only in developing new skills but also in the chance it provides for staff and carers with similar problems to meet, talk and get support from one another. If your Home is seen as a good training centre, you will be more likely to attract good staff. You believe in quality of work and the quality of life of older people. This can only be good for business as well.

Training for senior staff

This is an area where you may be able to share and exchange your own expertise with other Homes or bring in outside trainers. Many senior staff are working for NVQs/SNVQs at Level 3. Topics that would be helpful are:

- Communication skills
- Using an induction pack
- New developments in the treatment of mental and physical disability
- Assessing staff for NVQs

Questions to consider

- Find out whether other Home owners would be interested in taking part.
- Make a list of suitable topics for training and people able to run the courses.
- What would the costs be?
- What are local colleges offering?

Steps to take

- Design in outline a training programme for senior staff.
- Talk to the staff of your local social services Training Department.
- Set up a trial course to see if it is beneficial and cost-effective.

Training for care assistants

The quality of care in your Home is bound up with the quality of training you give to the people who work in it. Managers have found that the NVQs and SNVQs are beginning to give care assistants a new status and pride in their work and so they are working as a team in a new way. There are a number of areas in which you could offer good training to a wider group of care staff or to other Home managers. You could offer a series of lectures or a complete training course in one or more aspects of care work. A typical course might include:

- The aims and philosophy of care for older people
- How to relate to older people with mental illness, confusion or physical disabilities
- Working with a care plan
- Residents' rights
- Dealing with forms
- Health and safety at work, and fire regulations
- Death in a Home with dignity

Questions to consider

- Would other Home owners be interested in taking part?
- Can you provide people who can act as trainers?
- What are local colleges offering?

Steps to take

- Make a list of suitable topics for training and people able to act as trainers.
- Design some training sessions that could be given by you or your staff.
- Set up a trial course to test demand and to check costs.

Training for carers

This may be something you could offer on a regular basis either for individual fees or through a group. Such a scheme would bring carers up to date with new developments on the management of care. It could also offer them a chance for support and to meet each other over a cup of tea or coffee at the session. It could be the start of a valuable carers' group in your area. If there already is such a group, they may be willing to help organise and/or pay for such events.

Training for carers can also provide continuity of methods of care if their relative comes into the Home for a respite break. One Home invites carers to spend some time observing how the care is given during respite care, so that when the older person returns home new ideas are carried on.

Carer training will introduce carers to the services your Home offers and it may also lead to their relatives coming in for respite or long-stay residential care. The range of topics for carers could include:

- Lifting techniques
- Diet for the older person
- Managing incontinence
- Managing poor memory and confusion
- Dressing leg ulcers and other wounds
- First aid in the home

Questions to consider

- Talk over the idea with the local social services team manager.
- Ask if they know of a carers' group in your area.
- Consult carers whom you know about the topics they would find helpful.

KEY POINTS

- Your business consists of people as well as bricks and mortar.
- Consider upgrading your premises as a first step to diversification.
- Using your Home as a social, care or training centre will enrich your staff as well as the community.
- It could also make good business sense by attracting long-term residents.

TAKING CARE INTO THE COMMUNITY

This is really an extension of care within the Home. It is not a substitute for filling empty rooms, but it may provide a way for you to develop the business in the future. There are a number of services that you may be able to provide: for example, a 'night sitting' service, holiday care in someone's home, doing odd jobs around the house. (These are covered in more detail in the next chapter.) It may also be helpful for staff who work full time in a Home to go out from time to time, and it is also good for them to see older people as individuals in their own homes. Links are established that may lead to domiciliary clients becoming long-stay residents – your Home will provide them with a 'seamless service'.

From a business point of view, it may be best to run domiciliary care as separate enterprise. Care in a residential Home is not registered for VAT, but you would have to register for services outside the Home if your turnover were above the current (1994) threshold of £45,000 a year. This will affect the price you can charge. If domiciliary care is set up as a separate business, you will not have to include many overheads from the running of the Home. For more on this see page 105.

Setting up a home care service – the petal principle

This is a method of starting up a new service starting from a small base. The Home acts as the centre of a flower with petals radiating out from the centre. You start out with one petal and demand will tell you which petal to go for next.

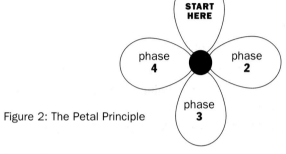

Figure 2: The Petal Principle

The idea is to operate in only one geographical area from the Home rather than in an all-round radius. This system has several advantages:

- Transport costs are minimised.
- You do not over-extend your services.
- You have the chance to see if it works out.
- You can build up clients and loyalty steadily.
- People in a small neighbourhood are more likely to hear about your scheme and tell others about it.

If the idea is a success, you will find that people living nearby will begin to ask for a similar service. You will then be able to start on another petal and so on.

Staffing

To the recipient, having someone in for a domiciliary service is a bit like bringing in someone to do odd jobs, but with a difference – the person receiving them has to be assured of continuity in the quality of the work. Older people are among the most vulnerable in the community so it is essential that you are able to trust a person whom you send into their homes whatever the service that is to be carried out. Induction, training and references will be necessary. You yourself will need to monitor what they do, and make sure they know about it and receive feedback (see Chapter 7).

What care or services should you offer?

You may prefer to start just with personal care in bathing and dressing and making a light meal. However, there are always other things that seem to need doing such as changing a light bulb, getting in some more catfood, and the carpet needs a hoover and what about changing the sheets? Many older people will worry about a lawn that looks untidy when the grass is long. These are problems in their lives that a carer is often glad to hand over for a time, or that someone living alone may prefer to pay for rather than going into a residential Home.

You will also need to decide whether to go for a private market, or whether you may want to tender for an SSD contract. In the latter case, you will have to comply with the SSD requirements. A comprehensive home care service could include:

- full personal care during the day, evening and night
- light meals prepared on the premises or brought to the house
- cleaning, dusting and bedmaking
- household jobs
- a sitting service
- looking after pets: feeding the cat, walking the dog
- tidying the garden, cutting the grass.

Questions to consider

- Ask your local social services care managers how much care they propose to purchase from the independent sector in the next year.
- Do they offer spot or block contracts (see Glossary)?
- Do they have an accreditation system, or standards they expect providers to meet?
- Consider the area in which you could offer a service on the petal principle.
- What is the competition?
- Offer your own version of a spot contract to staff for individual hours rather than full-time work.
- Think about how to market the service.

Steps to take

- Amend the contract of service with your own trained staff so that you may call on them to work inside or outside the Home.

- Recruit a further team of part-time workers who are prepared to work evenings and weekends. Make sure that you have more than enough to cover jobs. You will need a trained bank of potential assistants/outworkers.

- Carry out comprehensive training in the Home before you send staff out into the community.

- Offer spot contracts for individual hours rather than full-time work.

NOTE   A service of this nature is one of the most common ways in which a Home can diversify. It will need energy, commitment, hard work and the ability to cope with disappointment. Be sure, also, that any expansion you make is not at the expense of your core business, residential care; otherwise, the quality on both sides will suffer. If diversification is an option that you want to take seriously, you will have to have taken stock of your own qualities, the business as a whole, staffing and training and the problems of marketing. Other chapters will help with all these aspects of diversifying in more detail.

Operating a franchise

There is a further way of moving into domiciliary care. This is to operate a franchised package of care that has been devised by a specialist organisation. A reputable home care agency will offer good business thinking combined with steps to make sure that all the care is of high quality. You should look for a franchise operator that will:

- Give advice and training on setting up a domiciliary service.

- Assist in making and maintaining good links with the contracting social services departments, health authorities and GPs.

- Work to a code of practice.

- Assist in recruiting, assessing and monitoring the work of care assistants.

- Assist in marketing.

- Operate to an approved standard of service such as BS 5750 or the new Investment in People initiative.

As a franchise holder, you will be expected to operate to the standards of care set down by the operator. There may be some aspects that you may not have considered. For instance, the care package may include 24-hour emergency service through an alarm system linked to private homes. An emergency alarm must have a quick response if it is to be effective. Would you be willing and able to provide this? Furthermore, are you aware that a franchise may be expensive to run and that you will have to pay for it out of profits in an area that is not in itself very profitable?

Developing your specialist skills or interests

Many people who run residential Homes have come from another career and have a number of skills – there is probably no such person as a typical proprietor. No doubt your energies have been occupied in management or care, but do you have other talents or skills that you could use to add to the services already offered in your residential Home?

This section includes things that you do already which you take for granted. However, business opportunities often start from interests and hobbies. Perhaps you could develop your expertise and act as a consultant for older people living at home or their carers. Your skills might include cooking and diet, special care, gardening, etc.

Diet and nutrition

As you will know, older people have slightly different needs from those of younger people. If they live at home, however, they or their carers often continue to cook the same kind of food as they have always had. The diet may not include sufficient fibre, fruit and vegetables. You have probably learnt a good deal about the kind of food that older people enjoy and that is good for them. Can you develop that knowledge? You could offer:

- A regular or occasional meal service either at the Home or delivered.
- Advice on diet either in their own home or through classes for carers.

Questions to consider

- There are a number of regulations about the transport of cooked food. You will need to comply with them.
- Are you sure you can always provide a regular service?

- Some local authorities now offer frozen meals delivered once a week to their clients, who can choose from a wide menu. Would this option attract you?

Gardening

Many residential Homes have attractive gardens. You may be an expert on easy-care gardening and know a lot about plants and shrubs that a disabled person could look after at home. Do you enjoy planning a garden? Are there older people in your area who could do with some specialist advice on adapting their gardens? You could offer:

- A personal advisory service.
- Assistance in looking after it as part of a fuller domiciliary service.

Questions to consider

If you believe you could follow up either of these suggestions, or have other skills you could develop, decide whether they should be:

- Offered on their own
- Offered as part of a wider domiciliary service
- Included as part of a training programme for carers

KEY POINTS

- An advisory group can provide you with support as well as ideas.
- Use skills and talents as well as premises.
- Get advice from your local authority.

4 Changing the Nature of the Business

The forecasts may be true – 30–50 per cent of independent residential and nursing Homes may go out of business over the next few years. If this happens, there could be many large houses up for sale at the same time. If you think you may be forced to close and you decide not to diversify in the ways suggested earlier, you may wish to consider other ways of making use of your property. Further advice on closure is given in Appendix 1.

Note that all the suggestions outlined below assume that you will decide to close down the business as a residential Home and that your older residents will not be expected to share their home with another group of people. Many of the ideas are far reaching – they will need capital, energy and commitment.

OFFERING ACCOMMODATION FOR A DIFFERENT AGE GROUP

It may be possible to offer accommodation to a different clientele but this depends very much on where you are situated. Large houses in areas where there are active older people, tourists or students may be converted into sheltered housing, small hotels, bed and breakfast or even student hostels. Each of these will demand different standards of accommodation and service. You will need fewer staff but the costs of making the conversion may be high. If you do decide to move out of residential care as such, you will need to consult and prepare your long-term residents as you would for closure.

Sheltered accommodation

The first option is to offer sheltered accommodation without care for older people whose health is reasonably good. It may not be as difficult as you think to make up sets of rooms in your Home, each with its own bedroom and sitting room, a small kitchen and a bathroom en suite. You will already have public reception rooms, laundry facilities, etc. Conversions will cost you money, but will it be a much higher cost than upgrading individual rooms? You will save on food and upkeep. You will need far fewer staff to run the place, perhaps only a warden who can call on local agency help on an ad hoc basis. Sheltered housing is worth considering if you are in an area large enough to support a number of active older people who like to be independent but can call on care services in an emergency.

However, before you begin even to make plans in your mind you must obtain sound financial advice on the overall viability of providing sheltered accommodation. It may be that there is more need for sheltered accommodation where carers' assistants are employed by the agency that operates the service. This of course means additional cost.

Questions to consider

- Find out about the demographic spread of older active people in your area and their estimated income.

- Talk to the local inspection and registration unit to make sure you will not need to fulfil registration criteria.

- Look seriously at the structure of your Home to see if it makes sense to offer sheltered housing service.

- Work out how many units you could provide.

- If you are also considering upgrading the property, ask for further quotes on making up sets of apartments.

- Consider whether you offer flats to rent or to buy.

- Find out what Housing Benefit would be paid.

NOTE There is over-provision of sheltered housing in some areas. Is this true in yours? Find out about the competition.

Hotel or bed and breakfast

You should be able to find out from your nearest tourist information centre about the possibilities of starting up a small hotel or bed and breakfast (B&B) in your area. Are there others in your neighbourhood already? Will the market sustain more?

NOTE The term 'tourist' is used for anyone who spends a night away from their home town. It includes people on business as well as pleasure. You may also like to consider offering facilities as a small scale conference centre. You may not wish to compete with the plush surroundings of the local top hotel, but many conferences are held at a more modest level. This is something to take up with your local training board and the tourism section of your local council or authority.

Questions to consider

It is difficult to offer specific advice because what may be possible depends so much on where the Home is placed. Points to consider are:

- Is your Home in an area where there is a large tourist population?
- Do they come for the sights or on business?
- What are the different requirements – will fax machines or a welcoming open fire be more popular?
- Can you find out from the town hall what tourists spend on accommodation, on average?
- Is B&B a better option than a small hotel?
- How would you find your clients?

Student accommodation

Students needing accommodation are not only British. In many parts of the country there are foreign language students here to study English. As they are away from their own country they are usually responsible in their behaviour and very grateful if a landlord makes them feel at home. This, of course, is something that Home owners are used to doing. Accommodation for mature or married college or university students is also often hard to find and it could make sense to set up a student hostel of rooms or studio flats with a resident warden.

Questions to consider

- Consult the accommodation officer of local colleges or universities. What is the student population?
- Is there a need for places for them to live? What is the going rate?
- Consult the accommodation officer of language schools in your area. What are their special needs? Could you provide for them?
- Can you regain possession of your property if necessary? Check the legal position on tenancy or licensing agreements very carefully.

HOSPICE CARE

This is a very specialised area but one that gives a great service to the community. If you have a nursing background and run a nursing Home or a dual registered Home, you may be drawn towards exploring the possibilities of offering short-term care for people who are terminally ill and who may be in a great deal of pain and suffering. The hospice movement covers home care, day care and in-patient care. There are upwards of 200 hospice units in the United Kingdom. Some are large and may have separate nursing home and day care wings. The smaller ones, from around ten to twenty beds, run best alongside day and home care, which ensures that the medical input is adequate.

There are important differences between a hospice and a nursing Home.

- The length of stay in a hospice is short – usually not more than three weeks.
- A hospice has a strong medical team, which includes a doctor with experience of palliative care and symptom control, in addition to nursing and care staff.
- A hospice will provide intensive outreach support for patients in their own homes.

Dame Cicely Saunders, who founded St Christopher's Hospice in south London, the first modern hospice, explains what lies at the heart of their care.

Cicely Saunders 'We are caring for people whose illness is no longer going to respond to curative treatment. We try to offer control of symptoms. Often we are dealing with family crises, and as far as possible we aim at having people in their own homes for as long as they can manage.

'People from a hospice background look at the whole person and there is always input from pastoral or spiritual care, a skilled social worker as well as the medical staff. It is an interdisciplinary team. At the core is good nursing, but it is nursing that is concerned with people's potential at the end of their lives. People can do an enormous amount with reconciliation with family, with themselves and what they've done and use the time really creatively.

'Hospice is about living until you die, as fully as you can and as truly your-self as you can. We encourage that from the moment of admission or the first visit to a person's home. We listen to the family as well as the patient. The family is seen as the whole unit of care.

'We work as much by indirect attitude as by direct suggestion – "It's good to meet you now". Staff have a role in listening. If terminally ill patients start talking about their lives, they can begin to look at them in a different way. Having been is a very important part of being.'

The Hospice Information Service (details in the 'Useful Addresses' section) has prepared a pack of information for anyone who is considering whether and how to set up a hospice or palliative care service. They also advise that you consult your local health authority at an early stage and discuss the project right from the beginning. Your own area may need one of more the following:

- home care
- day care as a back-up to home care
- in-patient care.

Steps to take

- Send for and study the information pack mentioned above.
- Visit local hospices or palliative care services.
- Consider carefully whether you have the necessary commitment and personal qualities necessary.
- Consult local medical and health authorities, including GPs and consultants in local hospitals.
- Consult professional associations working in hospice care (see p 135).

- Check out possible sources of funding. This is essential, because hospice care is expensive and is not funded by a social services department as part of normal community care.

If you still believe this is a service you would like to provide, study the practical steps suggested in the Hospice Information Pack.

CLOSING DOWN COMPLETELY – CUTTING YOUR LOSSES

Closing down a residential or nursing Home is a drastic step, as it is in any business. Those who have been involved with closures believe that it is essential to organise the closure in an ordered way and to work with the local SSD. Appendix 1 is based on a document drawn up by Oxfordshire County Council, which closed down five of their Homes over a period of two years. Although the closure of a Home inevitably arouses considerable anxiety, the experience of Oxfordshire County Council indicates that, if the issues are addressed in an open and honest way with staff, residents and relatives, the stress of closure can be significantly reduced.

KEY POINTS

- Don't just go for the obvious alternatives – look around the problem.
- Be realistic in your approach.
- It is important not to rush into major changes.
- Use the talents and experience of your staff and associates.
- Work to a timetable.

5 Moving On

Up to now this book has looked at the background to the need to diversify, what the options are and what they may involve. If you have had an honest look at the state of your establishment and decided to go further, you will need to start spending money and time in setting up some serious market research and drawing up a business plan.

Residential Home owner 'You finally get to the stage when you start looking ahead and realise that you have got to do something. That's the moment when it starts to get hard. You must never under-estimate how hard it's going to be. Not just changing the business, but letting go of the old one. I still find it hard not to jump in when I see my manager doing something in not quite the way I would do it.'

This chapter takes you through these stages of moving into the new business in some detail, starting with the research into the possibilities ahead.

LOOKING AT THE MARKET

The viability of a business depends, as all Home owners will be aware, on the current and future state of the market. You will need to look hard at your marketing strategy, carry out market research and develop a marketing plan. As with many of the suggestions in this book, it is part of the whole process of taking stock.

Market research is a specialised area. You may try to do it yourself, or you may prefer to go to a market research agency. The next section is based on a market research plan carried out by a small to medium sized

Home. It includes a briefing document and a resumé from the final research report.

Sample brief to the Market Research Agency

We wish to establish the commercial viability of establishing a private community care service for disabled and elderly people within an eight mile radius of Anytown/district. As one of the partners of the Home is a registered general nurse, we intend to include nursing as well as care services. Proposed services to be offered include domiciliary help, day care and emergency call service.

- We need to assess the number of people over the age of 70 years in the catchment area and their socio-economic status, including cluster groups.

- We need to establish the sort of services they need and would be prepared to pay for. Is this segment growing or decreasing?

- We need to evaluate the competitive activity in the local area, to include all independent and voluntary organisations, private nursing agencies and charities that offer home support:
  Size and profitability
  Services offered, and where
  The hours of business
  The following organisations operate in this line of business:
  Voluntary organisations
  Profit-making agencies

- We need to establish how a private community care service would be perceived by:
  client group
  GPs
  DSS
  NHS providers
  local authority SSD
  voluntary sector

- We need to explore alternative sources of funding.
  The domiciliary service estimated at £X per hour is:

Domestic help

Housework, shopping, cooking, laundry.

Possibly gardening and a 'meals on wheels' provision.

Personal care

Mobilising, getting up and putting to bed, bathing, hair washing, hand and foot care, day and night sitting services.

Social help

Transport, outings, shopping, reading and writing, visits to doctors, hospitals, opticians, chiropody etc.

Emergency call service

A 24-hour service for attendance at the client's own home at a cost to be advised.

Questionnaire

Part of the research should be a questionnaire. Below is a draft of the type of questions that should be asked of the target client group.

WHAT SORT OF HELP DO YOU NEED?

- Security – *personal alarm call system linked to local service*
- Companionship – *outings, activities, sitting service, visits to doctor etc, holidays, day care*
- Domestic tasks – *shopping, meal preparation, cleaning, laundry, gardening*
- Personal care – *lifting and moving, physiotherapy, managing incontinence, handling medication, chiropody*
- Nursing care – *dressings, care of pressure areas, injections, catheter care, other specialised help (please specify)*

HOW OFTEN?

- Daily – *one or more hours*
- Weekly – *a few hours*
- Overnight – *regularly: how many nights per week?*
- Occasionally
- Round the clock care:
  few days a week, permanently/occasionally
  few days a month, permanently/occasionally
  emergency only

DAY CARE

Would you be interested in a day care service?

- Every day
- Regular days a week
- Occasionally

AN EMERGENCY CALL SERVICE

Have you considered one of these?

If you have one, is it reliable?

Would you like it to be linked with a Home that you know?

Market research report

The final report from the marketing agency was a comprehensive break-down of the current provision of private and fee-paying organisations, voluntary organisations and health authority or SSD services. A summary of the findings is given below.

Private and fee-paying organisations

There were six operators in this field, who offered care in different combinations.

Nursing care

Two organisations offered comprehensive nursing care. The report listed their services and fees for day and night nursing support as well as a sleeping-in service.

Nursing and social care

Several agencies offered social as well as nursing care and also domestic services. Each agency was listed, together with its services and fees.

Other

There were facilities for active elderly people at a local health and fitness club.

Charities and voluntary organisations

The report listed 19 such organisations with strong local branches or representation. They included sheltered housing provision, church groups and societies for older people, including Age Concern. The provision and range of care offered varied widely and there were no overall common factors.

NOTE This sector is developing rapidly in many areas of the country and has already established strong links with local SSDs. It could be a major source of competition for a small service that needs to make a profit.

Government schemes and SSDs

The report listed other providers of care services run through schemes such as the Probation Service. It also included day care provision in local authority Homes and the range of nursing and home care services operated by the health authorities and SSD.

NOTE Much of this care is now channelled through SSD care managers. This is an area where you should be dealing directly with the department concerned rather than through a market research team (see below).

Your own research

As part of your market research package, make a formal assessment of the information you have gathered to date about the local community care provided in your area.

SSD, health authority, health centres, GPs etc

- Do they know about your Home?
- Have they visited it recently?
- If not, issue an invitation.
- What are their overall requirements for the forthcoming year?
- What are their criteria for recommending services for private clients?
- What would you need to do to make your services acceptable?

Are you up to date with new legislation?

Apart from Community Care and Registration law, you should make sure you know about new regulations concerning:

- health and safety
- food hygiene
- fire regulations
- EC directives

KEY POINTS

- Consider commissioning a professional market research report.
- Make sure that you give the research company a well prepared brief.
- Restrict their research to areas where research could be time-consuming and difficult for you.
- Do your own market research in areas to which you have easy/personal access.

THE FINANCIAL SIDE OF YOUR BUSINESS

As anyone running a business knows, the 'bottom line' is that it has to make a profit. This section looks at the financial side of diversification, starting with the kind of questions a bank manager will ask. These are very likely the same questions they put when you set up your Home in the first place.

All the major banks have a specialist business service, usually at one of their larger branches. They will give advice to anyone considering developing or changing their business focus, and there are a number of useful leaflets to start you thinking. Here is a typical list of questions that banks or TECs suggest that their customers ask themselves.

- Where are you now?
- Where are you going?
- Have you the ability to get there?

- How are you going to do it?
- How much will it cost?
- How much will you get out of it?
- Is it all worth while?
- Is capital or revenue more important?
- What are the risks?
- What is your marketing budget?
- What is your pricing policy?
- What is the finance required?

Making 'what if' projections

This is a useful method of estimating the income and costs of a number of different enterprises. It can be done with a good software package such as Lotus 123 or SuperCalc. The package provides the framework for the questions you need to ask and you can then enter a number of different permutations about each area of potential diversification in terms of finance and resources.

Questions to consider

- You decide to upgrade the facilities of the Home. What price do you need to charge to cover the costs?
- You are considering taking in residents who need a high level of care. The social service funding will bring you £X for each such resident. Your extra costs in staff and training will be £Y. What, if anything, is the profit margin?
- You want to set up a home care business. What is the going rate in the private and local authority sectors per visit? What income do you need to generate to cover the costs of part-time care staff? What extra costs such as transport and training will you need to build in, or do you already have the capacity to cover these? What are the profit margins?
- Will it be better to diversify now, or can you afford to wait for a while, or should you cut your losses and close the business?
- Will new services attract long-stay residents and help advertise the Home?

- Are you prepared to break even or make a loss in the short term in order to attract new long-stay clients?

Business plan

When you have examined these options you should be in a position to consider your business plan. A well thought out document is the first stage in total planning. It will show clearly the aims of the business, sometimes called its philosophy or 'Vision' (see p 29), a review of the market, a financial projection and a cash flow forecast. Finally the business plan will set down how you are going to achieve your goals – your 'Mission statement'.

A business plan provides evidence that you have given careful thought to the undertaking, even if some of the forecasts are provisional. After completing a plan, check through it carefully to see whom you should now consult further. Names and addresses of some organisations that can help are given in the section 'Useful Addresses' at the end of the book.

The business plan outlined below is based on one drawn up by an independent Home that has successfully diversified over a two-year period. It is important to stress that they did not attempt to diversify without a very thorough survey of the market, as discussed later.

You could use this plan as a basic model. You can also obtain samples of business plans from the major banks or other financial advisers. You may find it most appropriate to tailor your own document from several examples.

SAMPLE BUSINESS PLAN

The business idea

We have successfully established a Care Home for older people, Ocean View House,[2] near the town of Anytown. We have now identified a need for further residential care in these areas:

1. For older people to obtain respite care or holiday relief.
2. To support older people after a stay in hospital, before returning to their own home.
3. Long-term care for frail older people.
4. Long-term care for older people with mental confusion/dementia.

We have also identified a need to supplement home help and warden support for older people living in their own homes.

- One of the effects of the 1990 Care in the Community Act has been that the amount and levels of care given to people at home are much higher than previously.

- Community care services given through the NHS and the local authority social services are increasingly being contracted out.

- The services provided by the social services are not always comprehensive. Elderly people are often inadequately supported, especially at weekends and at night times.

- Even where there are sufficient local authority resources, some older people prefer and are able to make their own arrangements and provision from private income.

Mission statement

To support elderly or disabled persons in their own homes by the provision of a reasonably priced, quality assured range of personal, domestic and social care, tailored to their needs. To support them further by holiday relief and day care services based at Ocean View House.[2]

Business name

Green Fields Home Care Service[2]

NOTE This is to be kept separate from the business name of the residential home, Ocean View House.[2] The new business will be managed by one of the partners as a separate enterprise.

The local area

Anytown is situated in a [rural/urban/suburban] area. There are many older residents who are reasonably affluent or who own property. Many of them are retired professionals with a high expectation both of longevity and of quality of life.

- A flexible private provision of domestic, personal and emotional and nursing care would allow them to remain in control in their homes for a longer time.

- It would also allow families to remain together by supporting this care with holiday breaks and day care facilities at Ocean View House.

- By developing a good relationship with older people in the neighbourhood, we would be able to offer a less traumatic and hopefully happier transition to full-time residential care if this should become necessary.

Reasons to expect a successful outcome

- The increasing age of the population.
- The increasing age of the elderly population.

[2] The Names of the Homes are invented and have no connection with real Homes of this name.

- The current gaps in the service provided by the NHS, social services and voluntary sectors.

- The greater number of people receiving Community Care.

- The need that has already been demonstrated by the residents and families in our Home and through a market research project (attached).

- The reduction in numbers and availability of family carers (through factors such as divorce and job mobility).

- The increasing number of people with private incomes above state pension level.

Managing the service

We believe that we have the right mix of management and care skills to run a successful home care service through:

- Our experience in health care and care of older people.

- The skilled staff who are already on hand.

- Our management systems that already exist.

In addition:

- Our proposal supports the Government plans for Care in the Community.

- We already have the confidence of GPs, the social services and hospitals in the area, including consultants.

Short-term objectives in the first year

We aim to achieve 25 per cent take-up of the total catchment area for the Home Care Service by twelve months after start-up and 25 per cent take-up of day care services in the second half of the first year.

Long-term objectives, three to five years

We aim to achieve 60 per cent take-up in both areas.

Long-term objectives, four to six years

It is our intention to expand into designated day care premises and rehabilitation services for older people.

Immediate tasks

- Identify the market and produce a computerised database.

- Assess details of local needs from previous research.

- Identify and cost the extra equipment needed.

- Produce a 'menu' of services offered and cost each one carefully.

- Contact local GPs, the social services and voluntary sectors. Inform them of the proposed service and ask for their current needs:
  who?
  what?
  when?
  where?

- Price the services.
- Identify staff required.
- Train staff.
- Raise the capital required.
- Buy and commission the equipment.
- Produce two brochures:
  for GPs, the social services and voluntary sectors
  for prospective clients and relatives of clients.

Finance required

We estimate that the amount required will be £00,000. Enclosed is a breakdown of individual expenses and the approximate time of expenditure.

We propose that the sum will be financed by:

- Financial institution source
- Private investor(s)
- Self/partnership
- Grants

We propose to repay the investment required over a term of XX years, repayable at annual interest of XX per cent.

Financial projection

Year One: fixed costs		
Vehicle		£00,000
Hoist		£0,000
Brochures and printing		£000
Advertising and PR		£000
Manager's salary		£00,000
	Total	**£00,000**

Year One: variable costs		
Staffing		£00,000
Consumables		£0,000
Transport		£0,000
Training		£0,000
	Projected income	**£000,000**

Year Two: fixed costs	
Second personal computer and laser printer	£0,000

Year Two: variable costs

Staffing	£00,000
Consumables	£0,000
Transport	£0,000
Training	£0,000
Projected income	**£000,000**

Past achievements

In 1984 we bought a property in Anytown and set up a twelve-bed care home for older people, which included renovating, staffing, equipping, marketing and management of a previously semi-derelict building. There was an extension to 19 beds by conversion into a properly appointed residential Home with larger care and staff facilities in 1987/88. The business was further extended in 1988/89 by building on four more bedrooms and incorporating a shaft lift, assisted care facilities and a laundry.

The Annual Accounts for last year are attached.

The extended service and enhanced facilities provide a home from home atmosphere which has been much appreciated by our residents. There has been 70 per cent occupancy of the Home – a figure in keeping with the age group concerned. It allows for redecoration and maintenance between each occupancy.

The current structure of the business

The partnership will continue to manage both arms of the business. One partner will be responsible for managing the new Green Fields Home Care business, with relief from senior staff of Ocean View Residential Home.

Initially the staff from Ocean View will be used to provide care, supported by a bank of care assistants, to be recruited. We have established that there are many people who live locally who can provide a few hours' service a week if the hours are flexible enough. We always have a large response to advertisements for part-time staff, but the hours do not always coincide with our permanent requirements. We will explore the possibilities of job-sharing for a group of care assistants.

Transport We intend to review this at an early stage to maintain flexibility. Some members of staff will use their own vehicles and will receive a mileage allowance.

Administration We see the appointment of a part-time secretary as an advantage but not as a critical necessity at this stage.

Target area We propose to work on the petal principle [see page 59], to minimise the risk of over-extending the business.

Professional advisers We shall continue to use the accountants, solicitors and bank facilities of the existing residential home business.

Appendix 1 of the business plan

Statistical evidence to support the business plan

- 14 per cent of adults look after someone who is mentally or physically disabled or frail
- the average age of carers is 45–64; one in five of this age group is therefore restricted and has less freedom to enjoy life than others
- 38 per cent are caring for 74 to 85 year olds
- 15 per cent are caring for 85+ year olds
- 33 per cent also have children
- 50 per cent also have jobs
- 20 per cent look after more than one person
- four out of ten carers are men.

In addition:

- 57 per cent of all carers spend 20 hours or more a week caring
- 8 per cent find it very difficult to get away for two hours
- 25 per cent have been caring for more than ten years.
- The person cared for may receive care visits from health, social or voluntary services.
- At any age an individual may be able to receive relief care from a paid attendant – but, in practice, only about 2 per cent do.
- The invalid care allowance is received by only 2 per cent of carers who are of working age.
- 66 per cent of carers who are over 65 and caring single-handedly get no help whatsoever.

Source: *Informal Carers*, Hazel Green, drawn from HMSO General Household Survey.

Appendix 2 of the business plan

Extracts from Anycounty local authority Community Care Plan

- As the Community Care Plan changes and develops over the next few years, we plan to alter the balance between the providers of residential and nursing home care (including the SSD's own direct provision) and community care services.
- We are already moving towards a mixed economy in the provision of care, and have the statutory duty to spend 85 per cent of the STG in the independent sector. This will lead to a significant increase in some areas of activity by the independent sector. Planning and development work has already begun.
- We have been collecting information about the domiciliary care service from relevant agencies and individuals. The following needs have been identified: *more choice for carers to be able to choose which part of the plan they can meet and which part should be covered by the domiciliary service; more flexibility in how services are provided and at what time of the day; the importance of maintaining standards of training and quality of care.*

We hope to be able to initiate a substantial increase in the level of expenditure for domiciliary care services in the next financial year. It may be possible to allocate some of the STG for domiciliary services for people with learning disabilities and a further sum for elderly people.

KEY POINTS

- A good business plan will tell the bank about your personal aims as well as those of your business.

- The more you are able to think through each option the better the chance of success.

- Be realistic in your ideas.

- Study your local Community Care Plan and Locality Plans and use appropriate extracts to back your case, if necessary.

6 Marketing and Tendering

MARKETING

By now, whatever option you have chosen (other than closing down or changing completely the nature of the business), you will have to consider how you are to market your new service. First, a useful fact: in a recession, those who continue to advertise throughout invariably increase their market share.

What is marketing?

The concept of marketing itself has come a long way from its origins. We tend to think of large companies with a director handling huge budgets and producing glossy brochures and TV ads. The language they use can be off-putting:

> 'Marketing is the management process responsible for identifying, anticipating and satisfying customer requirements profitably and effectively.'
> Institute of Marketing

It is a far cry – literally – from the bustle of a real market-place with its colourful stalls, the jostle of people, the cones full of turmeric or paprika (in a Middle Eastern market), while every stall-holder tries to convince you that their apples are the ripest and best value, their cooking pots will last the longest, their T-shirts are the latest fashion.

In marketing we need to keep both concepts in mind – the abstract words and the sales pitch of the real world.

Marketing means that in your real world you not only have to provide high quality care, you also have persuade purchasers that they need your product or service and why. You also have to persuade them that when they buy from you they are buying the best – at a reasonable price, of course. It may not be easy. So how do you go about it?

- You need to identify a gap in the market.
- You need to make sure that the services you offer are the ones the customers demand.
- You need to target your advertising and promotion at the right people.
- You need to be able to persuade people of their desire for your service – they may not want something until it is available.
- You need to present a good image.
- You need to be able to fulfil customers' expectations.
- You need to be ahead of the competition and establish a good reputation.

A good marketing strategy will take in all these factors. In today's world it is not enough to rely on a good reputation and word of mouth. Your successful competitors will also be in the market-place selling their wares. They may be subtle or they may be making a lot of noise, but they are being heard and seen. Are you? This chapter will help you to use your research and develop a marketing strategy through these areas:

Defining objectives

Budget

What your message is

How to get it across

The image you present

Objectives

In the sample business plan given in Chapter 5 there are three sets of objectives: for the first year, for the second year and for the longer term. They are very specific, aiming to reach a certain level of care provision in their chosen fields, rising from 25 per cent in Year One to 60 per cent in Year Five.

These are reasonable targets. The Home in the example propose to develop their business slowly, not to rush into things. This time-scale gives them a chance to correct their mistakes, to monitor performance and to build without over-stretching themselves. How do you define your objectives?

- for Year One?
- for Year Two?
- for Year Five?

Budget

You should already have estimated how much to spend on your marketing budget. Check it out again. You will need to include:

- Design and printing.
- Advertising.
- Simple ways of making the Home look more attractive – flowers, prints, a change of uniform (see below).
- Other (eg the cost of your time).

Your message

Content

It is essential to spend time in thinking about and defining exactly what it is you want to get across.

Unique selling point (USP)

This is the aspect of your business that makes you stand out from the rest. If you are the largest, then you will stress the benefits of that. The vehicle-hire firm Avis has built its business on not being the largest – so they 'try harder'. If your major competitor is a large medical insurance company, what can you offer that they cannot in the way of personal service or the 'try harder' factor?

Do you give better value for money?

Often, a smaller firm gives better service than a large one because they know the local area, they have a personal pride in being seen to do well and they have fewer overheads. Can you assure your purchasers that some of these apply to you?

How do you define your new service?

What makes your service different from that of your competitors? Perhaps it is:

- More personal and local – you will operate within a small area and be more responsive to individual needs.
- Better value for money – you do not have the overheads of a large agency.
- Well thought out – what you offer is what older people need.
- Reliable at all times.
- Well supervised and monitored.

Style

Consider the language you should use to get your message across, both face to face and in your literature. For this you must consider who is your target group and what kind of approach is most appropriate for them. They will probably fall into two categories – professionals and the general public, especially older people.

Social service department or nursing professionals

Professional people need to see a professional-looking approach. Your message should be up to date and show an understanding of the latest legislation.

When you talk to them, use their language (see the Glossary at the end of the book). They may talk in terms of 'enablers' or 'providers' and other jargon words. They may use initials as a short-cut. Obscure words are instruments of power, so know what they mean. It all helps to show that you are at their level – and are not intimidated.

Older people and their carers

You and your staff see older people every day. Take a moment to consider how you address your residents.

- Do you and your staff speak to them as equals or as children?
- Do you use their first names without consultation or do you ask how they would like to be addressed?
- Do you always include a resident in the conversation when talking about them with their relative present – rather than the 'does he take sugar' approach?

- Is it always clear that you and your staff respect their dignity, even though they may appear confused?

Presentation

You market your message in a number of ways – through face-to-face impressions, through brochures, by word of mouth and by advertising. This section goes through the different ways you can promote your Home to a wider public. Some of these you will have to pay for but you can also get publicity and become known through your own contacts.

Image – first impressions

Most of us judge on appearances. In fact, research has shown that up to 70 per cent of the impact of every product, person or institution is made at first sight. The book trade sells many books and magazines entirely on the impact of their covers. The sales rep goes round with a stack of front covers and if the subject matter appeals and/or the shop manager knows the name of the author, they buy it without a glance inside. And as the book often hasn't been written, this is just as well.

Obviously this will not apply so drastically in your field, but the principle still applies. A quick look round a Home will tell a visitor if the residents look reasonably happy and content, staff are willing to come up and talk to a stranger, the floors and walls are clean, there are no lingering smells and so on. Those are the basic levels.

- Does your Home achieve them?
- Are there areas that could be improved?

Moving up-market, a Home that also looks like a home – which of course it is for the residents – will score over one that looks or feels like an institution. Some nice looking pieces of furniture, pictures and flowers get their message over clearly.

- What is there in your Home that presents a friendly and homely image?
- What changes could you make to smarten or brighten it up?'
- Does the garden have accessible paths and seats?
- Are there attractive shrubs for all seasons?
- What could you do to improve the impression that visitors take away with them?

Brochures and stationery

A well thought out brochure in colour is the first way of telling prospective clients about your services. These are standard in every kind of organisation nowadays. Your brochure (or brochures if you propose to run more than one business) may be the first thing a prospective new client sees. The text for a sample brochure is shown in Appendix 2. Look at brochures of businesses in related areas such as small hotels or hospitals. Find a style that appeals to you.

With modern software programs you may be able to have one designed by someone you know if your budget is limited, but the ideal is to get all your brochures and stationery properly designed. If people are not tempted to pick up a brochure and read it, it is a wasted selling opportunity. As with the Home itself, a huge percentage of the success of your paperwork will be on first impressions. If you can write reasonably well and can set out the copy, shop around for a small design firm – as with other small businesses, they too are likely to try harder. A small printing company may be willing to do a deal. Shop around.

Tailor your brochure both to your existing clients and to potential new ones. It should be aimed both at care or nursing professionals and at older people and their carers. For instance, if you offer a good home for older people who are still fairly active, list the things that will make them feel stimulated and not bored. Show photographs of residents doing things or talking, not sitting in a circle watching television.

Describe yourself and your partners, your staff, your philosophy of care – everything that will tell a client that you have a quality service.

Keep it simple. It is cost-effective to have a glossy brochure that will last for a few years and a slip-in sheet giving prices and details that can be altered from year to year.

If you are moving into a different area of care, concentrate on things that the new client group will need. For instance, if your new service is for more dependent older people, you could mention:

- En-suite facilities (if you have them).
- Some typical rooms.
- Modern equipment.

- Modern methods of dealing with physical problems or difficulties such as pressure sores, incontinence and limited mobility.

- How you manage the care of older people with confusion or other mental health problems.

A separate brochure for day or home care services

If you propose to set up a new business taking care into the community or offering day care, you will probably need a separate brochure. Many people will want to keep this by their telephone for quick reference, so cut down on the pictures and aim at clarity:

- Use large type, so that older people can read it easily.

- Make it clear exactly what services you offer.

- Put the prices next to each service so that they don't have to refer to another document.

- Stress the ways in which you will monitor quality.

- Describe your philosophy of care, your organisation and the kind of people you employ.

- Show that you understand the need to be reliable. Older people often become distressed, as you will know, over being kept waiting or not knowing what is going to happen to them.

Advertising, PR and direct mail

Some ways of reaching prospective clients are suggested below. Which of them will be the most suitable will depend very much on your particular circumstances. Large organisations generally use three methods of marketing: advertising, public relations (PR) and direct mail. Small businesses should consider these options as well.

In a small neighbourhood, the parish magazine may reach your target audience. If you are in a large city, you may do better in mass media with a larger catchment area such as newspapers and local radio.

Home care manager 'We took out a television slot in the local hospital. They have screens now in a lot of departments with messages that flash up to tell the patients what's going on. It's quite expensive for them so they put in ads every ten minutes or so. It's not cheap for us, but it gets our name known. We're thinking of doing the same in the local Post Office queue.

We also put out leaflets into all the surgeries in our area and have had quite a good response.'

Steps to take

■ Advertising on local radio.

■ Putting small ads in local newspapers or parish magazines and in national magazines such as *The Lady* or *Community Care*.

■ Leafleting doctors' surgeries, other waiting rooms, libraries etc.

Public relations

There are a number of firms that specialise in PR and advertising. It may be worth paying for professional advice. The main purpose of good PR is to make yourself known and to tell people when you are doing something different.

Steps to take

■ Send out a press release to all local papers, voluntary agencies, carers' associations etc.

■ Talk to local voluntary groups.

■ Invite local choirs or entertainers to visit the Home.

■ Consider, with the agreement of staff and residents, having an open day or special launch where press and representatives of local organisations can visit the Home and be impressed with what you have done.

Direct mail

Large organisations consider that sending leaflets by mail is an effective way of generating business. The heart of good direct mail is a computer database that is properly targeted to the appropriate client base. There may be only a 5 per cent response to a mailshot sent out at random. A mailshot for a product or service that is correctly targeted may achieve a response of up to 25 per cent, so the experts say. Good direct marketing looks interesting and carries a message that the receiver will look at twice – and, hopefully, respond to.

Steps to take

■ Start putting together information about possible users of your services. Always list, where possible, a personal contact who can be addressed direct. (Remember that, under the Data Protection Act, you must have that person's permission to put their details on a computer database.)

- Make sure that you have a brochure or leaflet that gives your message clearly and is well designed.

- Write a covering letter explaining what you are now doing. Keep it brief, friendly but business-like.

- Find out from the Royal Mail about free mailshots for new businesses and whether this can apply to you.

- Send out a mailing in good time before your new services start (but not so early that you create an unsatisfied demand).

Your marketing strategy

When you have decided how you propose to market your services, you need to work out the steps that have to be taken to launch your new service. Make this as comprehensive as possible and include appropriate dates for each part. A run-down could look something like this:

PROPOSED LAUNCH OF NEW SERVICE 15 SEPTEMBER 1996

January 1996	Make provisional costings for each type of service
February	Copy for brochure
March	Get final estimates for alterations to day room/refreshing paintwork etc
April	Get builders in
May	Go through all figures with bank and accountant
	Proof of brochure
June	Decide on print run (number to be printed)
	Send brochures and stationery for printing
	Mail out brochures and covering letter in mail-shot
	Find suitable local celebrity to launch new service
July	Make sure all building work completed
	Take delivery of vehicle (if one is necessary)
	Check on uniforms etc
August	Send press release to local papers and radio
	Follow this with ads
	Take a break

September 1   Start induction training for new employees

Invite press, GPs, SSDs, nursing staff, carers etc to launch party

September 12   Check acceptances to party and finalise arrangements

---

KEY POINTS

- Marketing must be aimed in the right way at the right people.
- Know your objectives and target your strategy accordingly.
- Be able to talk to professionals in their own language.
- Address older people in a style that they will understand but is not patronising.
- The image your Home projects is one of your most important marketing tools.
- Design a separate brochure for each area of the business.

TENDERING AND CONTRACTING

Tendering for contracts

It is clear that over the next few years there will be many more residents in independent residential or nursing Homes who are funded through a contract with the local SSD. They will want quality care at a price that they can afford. From the Home owner's point of view, the care should be 'Up to a standard, not down to a price'.

The local authorities, through their contracting units and care managers, have a duty to obtain the best value for money in the independent sector. It is a buyer's market, so the contracts they offer will be on their terms.

As in other local and central government departments, the SSDs will ask providers of residential or home care to supply services either for a fixed, block contract or for a spot contract – which means that they ask you to carry out a service only when they need it.

Residential placements

Once you have agreed to sign a contract with the SSD, there is normally no negotiating – the SSD states its terms and you have to sign a binding agreement. This may seem a draconian way of doing business and it has been challenged in the County Court (see Note below). The Council has a duty to protect the rights of all residents that they pay for. If there is a dispute over the agreement, there is provision for an independent arbiter to look into the matter.

NOTE A recent court case involving Cleveland County Council and local care Homes was eventually decided in favour of the Homes. Although 'there was no reason in law why a local authority could not impose stricter contractual terms on a residential Home than was provided for by the Registered Homes Act 1984 . . . the duty to act reasonably required the council to consult, and if necessary negotiate, with Home owners on those terms and conditions.' *The Independent*, 30 December 1993.

At the time of writing, Cleveland County Council has decided to appeal against the judgment. However, whatever the outcome, if you and other Home owners in the area believe that your local authority is being unreasonable, you could have grounds for challenging them.

At the moment, many authorities make a new agreement with providers for each new placement in residential care. There is a move towards offering a general agreement which the Home owner or manager would sign and which would apply to every resident placed in that Home by the social services department. This would simplify paperwork, but it might mean that placements were restricted to a smaller number of quality care providers. If you want to apply to go on the SSD list but have not had much contact with them, you may need a marketing and PR drive to assure them that you provide quality care.

There will, nevertheless, still need to be an individual care plan for each resident in the Home, to determine what their particular needs are and how these are going to be met.

NOTE An individual should still have the right to choose to come to your Home even if it has not been placed on an approved list.

A typical agreement

Below are some points from the kind of agreement that you may be required to sign formally.

1   Prior to admission the Council will assess the needs of the Resident and agree with the Resident (wherever possible) and the Provider the 'Individual Care Plan'.

2   Before admission the Provider will have prepared a draft 'Provider Care Plan' which shall be prepared with information for the Council's Care Manager, the Resident (wherever possible) and a Third party (where appropriate). The Provider Care Plan shall be formally reviewed by the Provider within 14 days of admission, to include an appropriate level of detail to meet the needs of the Resident.

3   The Provider covenants to provide for the Resident's care and professional attention in accordance with the Council's care plan for that individual. Where a particular need is outside the immediate resources or expertise of the Provider, the Provider will promptly seek advice or assistance through the Resident's medical adviser or the Care Manager.

4   The Provider will treat all information personal to the Resident as confidential and not disclose any of it to any person who does not have a professional need to know or other legitimate interest in having it.

5   The Provider will not assign nor sub-contract any care or other services to which the Resident is entitled in whole or in part without the prior written consent of the Council.

Domiciliary care

This may be an area with more room to negotiate, depending on what your competitors have to offer. It is important to keep local care managers informed if you set up a home care service, so that they are aware not only of your existence but also of your special services. As local authorities differ, it is important to check what system operates in your own SSD. Many encourage potential providers to sit down and talk through the various options before they make a final decision to move into this area of care.

Because there is no statutory registration for domiciliary care, local authorities will have in place systems that fulfil a function similar to registration. The actual name may be different throughout the country, but the intention is to assure a quality care service. Providers will be placed on a list which may be termed one of the following:

- Voluntary Registration
- Accreditation
- Approved Status

  Sometimes voluntary registration is set up in conjunction with an overall 'umbrella' contract for providing domiciliary care; sometimes it is separate from the authority's contracting process.

  Some of the conditions that the SSD may specify in its contract agreements are set out in Appendix 3.

KEY POINTS

- Check SSD contracts carefully to make sure that you are willing and able to abide by them.
- Go for block rather than spot contracts if possible, for your own security.

7 Delivering the Goods

If you are reading this chapter, you will have thought through the various options, the problems you may encounter and how to cope with them, and are now well on the way to diversifying. This chapter is not going to tell you how to run a minibus to pick up residents for a day care service, but it may help you to check out your service so that you can run it in the best possible way. It will cover:

- Looking after the interests of your long-term residents.
- Settling in new residents, especially people who are more dependent.
- Keeping relatives informed and up to date with changes.
- Finding and contracting new staff.
- Making sure that you and your staff are properly trained to cope with the changes.
- Sorting out the different parts of your business – having the right systems.

SERVICE AS USUAL

You have a professional duty to make sure that any changes that you make in the Home, or to the way the business is run, are done with minimum disruption to your long-term residents. Remember that it is their home and that older people often find changes in their circumstances or surroundings very distressing. You should take steps to ensure that your staff are well briefed and that extra staff are around the Home when there are any changes that will have an impact on residents.

Planning for change

In Chapter 3 we suggested that you might like to set up a committee or working group to help you to make informed choices. You may find it useful to convene this group, or a similar one, to help plan the changes you have decided on – especially if they are likely to have a major impact on residents.

Alterations within the Home

This includes not only making structural alterations, which means workmen and builders around for some months, but also taking in a different, perhaps more dependent, client group.

You will need to inform the current residents and their families well in advance that changes are planned. Tell them either by letter or in person backed up by a friendly letter.

Steps to take

- Explain the nature of the changes.
- Explain the reasons for making changes.
- Explain how, if at all, they will affect the resident.
- If possible, keep at least one public room available for your current residents so that they will not have to be confronted by strangers – either for day care or for long-stay.
- Be prepared for an emotional reaction or even grief for apparent loss of life-style.
- Warn medical, psychiatric or nursing professionals of impending changes.
- Hold a group meeting of residents. If there is a residents' committee, work through them.
- Encourage families to increase their support over the period when the alterations are taking place.

Settling in new residents

You will already have a well laid down procedure for organising the care of a new resident. This will include helping them unpack, encouraging relatives to keep closely in touch, working with their care plan and monitoring their emotional and physical needs over the first few weeks (which is often a trial period). If, however, you are introducing several new people rather than just one or two, you may have to make extra provision so that the newcomers do not have to face any fears or resentment from other residents.

Steps to take or consider

- Organise a separate lounge, even if only as a temporary measure.
- Allocate members of staff to give the new residents support. A key worker system would help here.
- Hold a group meeting of new residents to talk about their reception – if this is possible.
- Monitor how the new residents are doing over the next few weeks even more than normal. Make a point of talking to them personally.
- Make sure that relatives and medical or nursing professionals tell you if they have any worries.

Introducing day care

How you will handle this will depend very much on whether you are building a separate day care unit or whether day care clients are to use the Home's facilities. As with introducing new long-term residents, you will need to keep your older residents and their families fully informed.

Steps to take

- Explain that you are going to operate a day care service.
- Explain the reasons for the new service.
- Explain how, if at all, it will affect the residents.
- If possible, keep at least one public room available for your current residents, so that they will not have to be confronted by strangers.
- Be prepared for an emotional reaction.
- Hold a meeting of residents to discuss your plans. If there is a residents' committee, work through them.

- Be aware at all times of the need to minimise disruption to residents.
- Let them know in advance about any changes you propose.
- If the changes are major, involve relatives well before alterations take place.
- Make sure that extra staff are on duty when any building work starts.
- If possible, plan to give 'old' residents some privacy from new or day care clients if they wish it.

A NEW HOME CARE SERVICE

If you have decided to start up a domiciliary service, your main set-up problems are likely to be in the areas of staffing, administration and predicting work load.

Staffing

Before moving to a different client group or setting up a home care service, you will have made sure that there are enough qualified staff in your neighbourhood who can operate the services as either full-time or part-time workers. You now have to check that they will work to your standards and to the expectations of the clients who will receive them. There are a number of ways you can do this.

References

There are some areas in which owners and future clients should, with reason, be particularly concerned. It is vital that you take up at least two references for any new member of staff, whether full- or part-time. This will help you assess that the applicant:

- is honest
- will not abuse a position of trust
- is a reliable time-keeper
- has the ability to understand the philosophy of the business and put it into practice when unsupervised.

Contracts

Contracts with part-time staff may not be as detailed as those for full-time staff, but they need to be reasonably comprehensive. Make sure that you include:

- The potential, but not the actual, hours of work per week that you may offer.
- Pay and conditions of service.
- A grievance or complaints procedure.
- A procedure that enables you to dismiss them if you have any reasonable doubts about their suitability. A trial period is usual.

Legal requirements

By law, if you are sending staff into someone's private home, you are responsible for assessing the risks to staff, even if you have a contract for care from the local authority. This means that you, or one of your senior staff, must visit that home personally to assess the risk element and make sure that it has been rectified. This includes, for example, faulty electrical fittings, loose stair carpets, dangerous gas appliances.

Local authority care managers will provide you with a care plan for any domiciliary care you provide on their behalf.

Induction

Each new member should have an induction pack which will set out:

- The philosophy of the service.
- A projected profile of the client group.
- Clear instructions about handling clients' money. *Note* this is a high-risk area.
- A job description, including conditions of service, grievance and complaints procedures, and a statement about confidentiality.
- A set of duty sheets, forms to be filled in for outreach work etc.
- An up-to-date set of regulations covering health and safety at work, fire and food hygiene.
- Special information about the Home or the neighbourhood.
- Travel arrangements.

Domestic or social care staff may also need information on:

- Transport of food.
- Laundry and cleaning methods.
- The proper disposal of waste materials.
- An appropriate diet for older people.
- Personal safety.

Training

Good-quality training is one of the major keys to a successful operation. It is something that the SSD will look for and expect to find. Again, you should already have some form of basic training in hand for your staff. What sort of training is it?

Questions to consider

- Are you familiar with the NVQ system?
- Do your staff work for NVQs?
- If so, what is the level they have reached?
- What other training do you give all new members of staff?
- How much refresher or in-service training do they get?
- When is the last time you yourself took time off to go on a training course?
- Can you get access to courses run by the SSD to help you 'speak their language'?

Training for domiciliary staff

Domiciliary staff are the people who represent your business to the general public. You need to make sure that they represent it in the best possible way. They should look professional and efficient, with clean and pressed uniforms, if worn. They will need most of the basic training that you already give your full-time staff. You may also decide to devise a further programme for part-time workers who will be going out on home care visits. Many of these are interpersonal skills and may include:

- Understanding the difference between providing care in a residential Home and in someone's own home.
- The importance of respecting how the client does things in their home.

- An understanding of the health needs as well as the social needs of older people.
- Listening skills: a person at home is often lonely and needs to have the opportunity to talk.
- The need at all times, as in your Home, to respect the client's dignity.
- The ability to act on their own initiative.

Supervision

Some Homes that have diversified ask all their part-time outworkers to spend two or three weeks in full-time service in the Home to see exactly how things are done and to brush up their skills in certain areas. This period also includes a training programme. Others, and this action may be recommended by the SSD, send out new care assistants with experienced staff from the Home for a trial period.

In addition, each new member of staff, full- or part-time, has a mentor – a more senior care assistant to whom they can turn for help or advice. You should encourage the mentor to keep an eye out for any problems, and also to come to you or a supervisor if the person seems to be having particular difficulty.

When a new member of staff goes on a domiciliary visit for the first time, send one of your experienced care assistants with them, partly to assist and partly to assess their suitability.

KEY POINTS

- Reliable and experienced staffing is the key to setting up a home care service.
- Set up systems from the start to monitor reliability and trustworthiness.
- Make sure that your contracts with staff allow for unsocial hours.
- Make sure that each part-time staff member projects the image and philosophy of the business.

ORGANISATION AND ADMINISTRATION

The general advice of those who have diversified successfully is to run each part of the business as a separate trading unit, whatever its status. The reasons for this are partly financial and partly to assist the organisation.

Financial advantages

One of the major reasons for this concerns VAT registration. Residential Homes are eligible to register to claim back VAT on certain goods – they do not charge it, of course, for care. The maximum amount claimable (gross) is £7200. If the figure is any higher than that the whole claim is disallowed.

If an owner diversifies the core business and buys equipment etc on which VAT can be claimed back, the figure of £7200 may well be exceeded. If the business is run as a separate company, the VAT registration number is also different and there is no maximum limit.

Manager 'We've found that a home care or day care service is likely to receive some of the income in cash as well as cheques. So if they're both registered separately, there's no danger that the finances of the two operations can become confused. The rules concerning VAT are quite complex – the simpler you make it for yourself, the easier it will be to keep the returns in order!'

The other advantage of running each service as a separate trading unit is that the owner can check easily the current state of the two businesses and make sure that one is not losing money and being subsidised by the other.

NOTE It is important that you consult your local Customs and Excise Office for the latest regulations on VAT. Whether you have to change this for a domiciliary service depends very much on whether you decide to operate as an introduction agency or as an employer. As an agency, you are a go-between for a self-employed person and someone who seeks their services. You provide no on-going support or training so you do not have to charge VAT on care services, only on your administrative costs. However, if you employ your own staff, you are obliged to charge your clients the current rate of VAT on all services that you offer – provided the turnover is above the current limit of £45,000. This obviously places quite a heavy burden on older people needing domiciliary care. You will have to balance the better quality associated with the support and training that you can give as an employer against the lower charges but not necessarily such consistent standards of care that an agency can offer. The location of your Home and the financial circumstances of the older people living nearby may be a deciding factor.

MANAGERIAL DIFFICULTIES

The major problem in setting up a new business, particularly if it runs beside an established residential care service, is keeping track of all the smaller parts. You will probably do best with a completely different office, a new telephone number and administrative support, even if this is only part-time. Then all the records can be held separately and, even if you employ some of the same staff in both areas, their different fields of work are treated as different jobs, unless you decide otherwise.

Before you start

You need to give yourself as much support as you can right from the beginning. For instance:

- Employ a separate manager to look after one of the businesses.

- If you want to concentrate your energies on the new business, appoint someone else to be in charge of the Home, even if it is only while you get the new service going. Clearly, if you do appoint a permanent or even an interim manager, you must make sure that they are up to the job and will satisfy all the stringent requirements of the registration and inspection unit.

Owner 'You have to realise how hard it is – starting a new business. You will have to commit yourself totally or you'll find yourself dragged between the old and the new business. When you're running a Home you become part of the furniture and to draw away from it is quite painful. But you have to accept other people's management of what you used to control.'

- Start from the beginning with proper computerised systems. Do not think so small that in a year you will have to key in dozens of records and data when you need to expand.

- Make detailed lists of all the services you propose to offer, with a cross-reference to those people who are able to do that particular job.

- Make another list, also with cross-references, of all the current and potential staff and their individual skills.

- Consider convening an advisory group from among users in your target area, including representatives of carers, older people and the SSD (if possible). Hold regular meetings so that you can discuss difficulties that arise, the best way of monitoring quality and whether the service is proving satisfactory. Let all your clients know informally that there is an advisory group, so that they too can make suggestions.

Using the computer

A well set up software program should also help streamline your administration in other areas:

- Work rotas
- Checking readily the availability of part-time assistants, especially at peak and unsocial hours
- Updating records
- Patterns of call-out for individual clients
- Record of menus, diet sheets and meals served if appropriate, as part of a domiciliary service
- Keeping up to date with new regulations
- Compiling a database of prospective users for marketing purposes (remember the Data Protection Act)
- And, of course, book-keeping and accounts.

KEY POINTS

- Do not neglect your own need for personal support and training when setting up a diversification service.

- If possible, delegate and find a support or advisory group to help.

- Keep essential records on the computer right from the start.

8 Final checks

You may in the end decide that it is better to improve your core business than to branch out. If so, there may be some ideas you could take from other people's experience that are related in this book. The most important are probably to make sure that your business is as efficient as possible, that you may do best if you provide a higher quality service and that you may be able to rethink or improve your marketing strategy.

If you have already taken the decision to diversify, the rest of this chapter may help remind you of what needs to be done and check out your own frame of mind while doing it.

Checklist 1 – your on ability to diversify

This is a major point for you to consider. However necessary change may be, it is often hard to carry out. Take a few moments to go through the following questions about the way you have tackled changes so far in your career, your life-style or the way you do things.

CAREER

I have

always been in the same line of business	☐
changed careers at least once	☐
had several different types of job	☐

LIFE-STYLE

I have always lived

in the same locality	☐
here and in one other place	☐
in several different parts of the country	☐

I like doing things

in the way they always have been done ☐

the way they will work best ☐

using new equipment and technology ☐

I enjoy the company

of my own age group ☐

of younger people ☐

of any age, if they are interesting ☐

I prefer to

keep to my own routine in the household ☐

share tasks where necessary ☐

do different kinds of job ☐

I plan holidays

well in advance ☐

on the spur of the moment ☐

EDUCATION

I have trained

in one type of business ☐

in at least two types of work ☐

and continue to retrain ☐

I believe that

you learn best from experience ☐

it is important to learn new ways of doing things ☐

Conclusions

Have a look at the answers that you ticked (there are no right or wrong ones, of course).

If you mostly ticked the first box of each section, it is likely that you are not a person to whom change comes easily. You need to think very hard and make sure you have adequate support if you propose to alter the nature of your business and make any major changes.

If you ticked the second or third boxes, or both, you have experienced change in your life, even if you haven't always wanted it. Think about the changes you ticked. Would you have preferred to do without them? If so, you should also think carefully about whether you could cope, or would want to cope, with changes now. The checklists below should help you.

Did changes come easily – in fact, do you rather enjoy making changes? If so, you should not find it frightening. You will need to make sure, though, that you proceed methodically and thoroughly, and do not rush into change without thinking through all the steps and making all the proper projections. The checklists below should help you.

Checklist 2 – the support available for you

PERSONAL SUPPORT

I am supported by

a husband, wife or partner	☐
good and caring senior staff	☐
a good team of assistants	☐
good administration back-up	☐
a religious organisation	☐
other	☐

PROFESSIONAL SUPPORT

I am supported by

the local SSD	☐
my bank manager	☐
my accountant	☐
a professional association	☐
other	☐

I need to find support from:

_____

_____

KEY POINTS

- Do you have the right personal qualities to diversify successfully?

- Do you have enough support?

- If not, can you find it?

- Have you set up an action committee or group as suggested in the last chapter?

Checklist 3 – planning: an overview

Before you make any important changes it may be helpful to stand back for a moment and make sure that you have allowed not only money but time as well to set them in motion properly. It may also be possible for you to try out some ideas before you commit yourself to them irrevocably. For instance, how would you and/or your staff actually feel when faced with a different client group? Could you cope with the emotional strain? If you propose to set up a domiciliary service, are you prepared to be rung up at 1am on a freezing January morning to organise help for someone who has had a crisis? A three-month trial period would give you a chance to see how you and your staff would cope in practice. Starting in a small way will also help ease a new service in gradually.

Have you worked out a detailed timetable for changes? ☐
Are you making change gradually and starting small? ☐
Will you make a trial run with a new service? ☐

Checklist 4 – staff and personnel

If you are going to diversify, inevitably much of your energies will be geared towards the new part of the business. So staff back-up will be particularly important in the early days. As suggested earlier, you may find it best to employ part-time care assistants who can offer a flexible service. You may also need to give them a different kind of training if you propose to move into caring for a more dependent clientele.

Your current staff

Have you discussed what is to happen and briefed them? ☐
Have they offered any suggestions? ☐
Have you made any changes to the way the Home is run? ☐
Do you propose to make any changes? ☐
Have you discussed it with all staff members? ☐
Have you worked out a training programme, if needed? ☐

New staff

How many extra/fewer staff will you need?   **How will you find them?**

Full-time _____   _____

Part-time _____   _____

Have you:	Yes	No
advertised?	☐	☐
interviewed?	☐	☐
checked references?	☐	☐
Have you worked out a training programme?	☐	☐

What are the core subjects?

_____

_____

	Yes	No
Have you drawn up a new contract of service?	☐	☐
Has it been agreed by prospective staff members?	☐	☐
Do you have enough senior staff or supervisors?	☐	☐

Checklist 5 – your permanent residents

Your residents will probably be affected in some way by any changes you decide to make. You will need to work out a strategy for informing them and their relatives.

	Yes	No
Are they aware of the changes you propose to make?	☐	☐
If necessary, will they have their own private room/s?	☐	☐
Have you organised staff to cover if workmen move in?	☐	☐
Has all alternative accommodation been agreed?	☐	☐

Checklist 6 – relationship with the local authority

Throughout this book we have stressed the importance of getting to know the people in the social services department and of finding out what the Community Care and Locality Plans are in your area. Be sure to keep the registration and inspection unit informed of any changes that you propose to make and also to seek their advice and views as they may affect the registration plans. Clearly, if you are mainly interested in a private clientele, some of the questions will not apply to you, but SSD officials believe that it is in the interests of all Home owners or managers to keep in regular contact with their local authority. You will, of course, need to consult the fire and health and safety officers as well as planning officers if you wish to change the use of part of your buildings.

	Yes	No
Have you seen the Community Care Plan?	☐	☐
Have you expressed interest in contributing to it?	☐	☐
Is there a Locality Plan in your area?	☐	☐
Do you know its main statements?	☐	☐
Will they probably be beneficial to you?	☐	☐
Do you know the names of people in the commissioning unit?	☐	☐
Do you know the names of local care managers?	☐	☐

	Yes	No
Have you met them personally?	☐	☐
If not, do you propose to make personal contact?	☐	☐
Have you talked over your plans with the inspection and registration unit?	☐	☐
Have you put in hand any changes they want?	☐	☐
Have you made sure that your plans are acceptable in terms of health and safety regulations?	☐	☐
Do you know who is on the Social Services Committee?	☐	☐
Have you ever attended any of their meetings?	☐	☐
Have you made contact with voluntary organisations?	☐	☐

Checklist 7 – finance

	Yes	No
Have you had a formal or informal meeting with the bank?	☐	☐
Have you worked out a clear business plan?	☐	☐
Have you made enough 'what if' projections?	☐	☐
Have you gone over all the figures yourself?	☐	☐
Have you asked an accountant to check them too?	☐	☐
Have you obtained several estimates for all work?	☐	☐
Have you arranged for all the capital required?	☐	☐
Have you costed all your proposed services?	☐	☐

Checklist 8 – the competition

As a result of your research, you should now have a good idea of how many other Homes or domiciliary agencies there are in your area, what kind of care they offer and which are in direct competition with you.

Residential Homes

There are _____ Homes in my locality. The breakdown is:

Type of Home	Number of beds	Client group
Private	_____	_____
Voluntary	_____	_____
Local authority	_____	_____

Domiciliary care

There are _____ businesses that provide a home care service in my locality.

The breakdown is:

Other residential Homes

Insurance companies

Private agencies

Voluntary agencies

Local authority teams

The services offered are:

_____

_____

_____

Checklist 9 – marketing

Marketing is always tricky because you do not want to create a demand that you are not able to fulfil but, on the other hand, if you do not advertise your services no one will know about them. However, whatever your final goal, it can do no harm to have a clear idea of what you want to sell, what you offer that is different from your competitors and what is the best way of reaching your potential customers, whether in the public sector or in a private market.

Are you happy with the message you want to give? ☐

Are you confident about your unique selling point? ☐

Have you had new brochures and stationery designed? ☐

Does your new image look good? ☐

Does an impartial observer agree? ☐

Have you worked out a marketing strategy? ☐

Have you made contact with all possible client sources? ☐

Checklist 10 – quality control

It is essential to have good feedback on how your new services are going. This can be given by word of mouth or through a questionnaire that clients are asked to fill in. If you have already employed a market research firm, they may be the best people to check with your clients, as a follow-up, how they rate your service.

What systems will you set up to monitor your services:

Personal visits to users? ☐

Questionnaires to users and purchasers? ☐

Other ☐

Checklist 11 – legal requirements

You must make quite sure that you have checked out all the legal side of sending staff into your clients' homes. Remember that the local authority will not take on risks, even if you are providing domiciliary care on their behalf.

Have all risks in private homes been properly assessed? ☐

Has the inspectorate or client agreed to make any
necessary alterations? ☐

Have you trained your staff to check for hazards such as fire? ☐

Checklist 12 – keeping up to date

The more you know what is going on in your area, the easier it will be for you to take advantage of developments or to influence them. As for many busy people, this is not always easy. How do you rate your knowledge of what is happening in the world of care both locally and nationally?

Do you read the local press regularly? ☐

Do you read reports of Council meetings and decisions? ☐

Do you lobby Councillors if necessary? ☐

Do you get magazines such as *Community Care*? ☐

KEY POINTS

- Take time to think through all the steps you will take.
- Anticipating a problem will go a long way to solving it.
- The more you plan ahead, the easier it is on the day.

Appendix 1

CLOSING DOWN A HOME

The plan given below goes through the procedure of closure in chrono-logical order. Smaller Homes may be able to cut down on the period of time and personnel involved, and may not be able to afford the quality described, but the progression may serve as a good model for any residential Home facing closure. It is not only you who are affected:

- Staff will have to look for new jobs.
- The social services inspection and registration team will need to check and agree on arrangements made for residents.
- Relatives or former carers will have to help residents choose another Home.
- Residents will have to come to terms with significant change in their lives.

Planning the closure well in advance is the key to success and it is essential to involve everyone who will be affected at early stage.

The roles of other organisations

The primary duty of care towards residents rests with the proprietor until the Home is closed. However, you must keep the registration and inspection unit informed – they will also be a source of advice. You should also inform the appropriate social services or health authorities as they may have financial responsibilities for some residents when a Home is to be closed; these are laid down in Local Authority Circular LAC(93)6. An extract from this Circular is given below.

'People over pensionable age in independent sector residential care Homes who face Home closure or eviction

'22 ... Local authorities will be able to make residential care arrangements for:

- people over pensionable age who

- have been evicted or are threatened with imminent eviction from a residential care Home (whether through Home closure or for other reasons).

'23 Regulation 9(2) of the attached regulations provides that local authorities will only be able to make residential accommodation arrangements for residents in residential care Homes who face eviction in a Home which is not owned or managed by the person or organisation which owns or manages the resident's current Home, unless the whole Home has been or is about to be closed down. This also applies where the resident has just been evicted from a Home. This is to prevent undue pressure being placed on local authorities to provide funding for residents with PR [preserved rights].

'24 Once a local authority has made arrangements for a person over pension age in a residential care Home, regulation 9(1) provides that the local authority will also be able to make arrangements to place them in a nursing Home if that later becomes necessary. If they are placed in a nursing Home and subsequently face eviction, regulation 9(2) provides that the local authority can only make further arrangements in accommodation which is not owned or managed by the person who owns or manages the current Home.

'25 It will be sensible for local authorities to draw up plans in the event that a residential care Home closes or a resident is evicted. With the local authority's advice and guidance, residents may be helped to find alternative accommodation using their PR without the local authority having to take financial responsibility for them. In drawing up such plans, the local authority will be able to ensure that arrangements for dealing with Home closures or evictions can be handled efficiently, with minimum distress to all residents. Such plans are likely to work most effectively if independent sector providers have been involved in their preparation. Similar arrangements should also be made in respect of nursing Homes.'

Closure steering committee or group

Set up a committee or group with representatives of all the people who are in contact with the Home in a personal or professional capacity. You could consider having a 'core' group and a 'full' group. Suggestions for membership include:

- the owner or manager

- representatives of
senior staff

care assistants
residents
relatives

- a financial adviser
- a social worker or care manager
- a member of the local health care team.

Suggested first agenda

1 Define the key tasks for closure. The areas may include:
Publicity
Support for resident/relative/staff
Timetable for closure
Transfer/Redeployment options and process.

These tasks can then be devolved to sub-groups to make up the full closure steering committee.

2 Set meeting dates from the present until after closure.

3 Ideally, you should identify an independent advocate (or advocates) who will represent residents. He or she should be involved with all the stages of closure from the planning onwards.

4 Ensure that there is adequate administrative/secretarial support. This person has a key co-ordination and support role.

5 Set in motion the preparation of letters or leaflets to confirm verbal announcements of closure. The group should agree to maintain confidentiality until a proper announcement of closure has been made to all concerned.

6 Plan how residents are to be told and by whom. Make staffing arrangements for extra cover on that day.

Announcing closure plans

Timing

- Plan to make an announcement about six months before closure, if possible.
- Discuss possible closure with the relevant authorities – DSS, SSD or health authority.

- Inform the staff first, so that they can support the residents.
- Inform the residents before the public.
- Consider the use of a press release after staff, residents and relatives know about the impending closure. This helps accurate information on closure to be published.
- Find out in confidence what vacancies may be available in other Homes.

Staff

- Managers should prepare for questions on pay and conditions, redeployment, redundancy etc.
- Consider inviting local trade union representatives to initial meetings and keep them involved.
- If you are running a large Home, use a variety of media to get the message across, such as briefing meetings, letters, leaflets etc.
- Arrange extra cover on the day of the announcement while staff come to terms with the situation; then arrange to tell the residents.

NOTE   You will need to beware of the spread of rumour and uncertainty. Tell and retell, because some people do not 'hear' the first or second time. Do not make promises that cannot be kept.

Residents

- Tell residents in groups or individually with their key workers as appropriate. Involve relatives at this stage if it is possible.
- Give out leaflets/brochures/letters with all the details of the options.
- Be clear about what alternatives can or cannot be offered, such as availability of options and the process of transfer.
- Allocate a key worker or member of senior staff to follow up every resident.
- Ensure that residents without relatives or friends have an advocate.

Relatives

- Consider each resident's views as to whether relatives or friends should or should not be informed.

- Inform relatives by phone or letter before the news becomes public knowledge. Careful timing is essential.

- Invite them to a meeting and personal interview within a week.

- Give out a leaflet, setting out the process, relatives' rights and complaints procedures. This should include financial information about where the local authority SSD can and cannot help and the cost of alternative care.

- Give details of the closure steering group, and inform and update them on developments.

- Arrange, with permission, for mutual support and exchange of addresses.

- Plan ahead for formal meetings to brief relatives on the progress of closure.

Personal support

Over the period of six months or so, everyone concerned with closure will need some form of support. This will not be easy, as one of the people most in need will be you as owner or manager. You will need to find your own support system from partner, friends or a professional association. The local authority or district health authority will be a worthwhile source of help in this difficult time.

Residents

- Allow extra time for staff to talk to residents, particularly in the days immediately after the announcement.

- Make it easy for relatives and friends to visit. Could you lay on special transport?

- Make sure that the people talking to residents – the key workers, an advocate and perhaps a social worker – know what their roles are and their boundaries; they must not promise things that cannot be delivered.

- Be prepared to work with or through relatives, where appropriate.

- Be prepared for significant emotional disturbance in some residents.

- Consider involving other professions, for example a geriatrician, psychologist or psychiatric social worker, psychiatrist.

- Consult and seek advice from the inspection and registration unit.

Staff

- Prepare as much as you can for practical questions about new jobs, money, transport, redundancy and so on. It may be helpful to talk to the social services care management team and also to local employment agencies.
- Give high priority to keeping up staff morale. They need support so that they can support residents in turn.
- Arrange different levels of support; for example groupwork, for staff to talk about feelings, and individual counselling, which may be formal or confidential.
- Be clear about maintaining confidentiality and about what they can be expected to do.
- Be prepared for significant feelings of loss arising from staff over relationships between residents and staff that will have to be broken off.
- Consider the use of an independent consultant – a therapist or counsellor – to assist staff, and also yourself.
- Involve trade unions if appropriate.
- If staff are not properly supported, they may leave too soon and the Home will be forced to close prematurely.

Relatives

- Involve relatives as much as possible in the closure procedure, if it is appropriate.
- Attempt to allay their fears that a resident will be 'dumped' on them, or anywhere else.
- Arrange or facilitate support groups.
- Prepare any Home that may be receiving your residents to give a sympathetic welcome to their relatives as well.
- Encourage relatives to keep in contact with an advocate or case worker.
- Help relatives to feel in control of the selection of the new place, and the timing of transfer.
- Be prepared to respond to the re-emergence of strong feelings, such as guilt or anger, from relatives about the original admissions.
- Be prepared to go fully into financial issues. This is likely to be a major problem in finding new placements. You should know who is likely to be

paying for a new placement: the DSS, local SSD, relatives or a combination of any or all of these. Your local contract/commissioning unit can advise you.

Relocation

You should begin to look at alternative places for residents and your staff as soon as you have made the decision to close down. Ask for a rough idea of preferences at an early stage. This may help the precise timing of closure if several vacancies may be needed in one receiving Home. A summary of procedures already mentioned and those you should undertake now is given below.

Checklist

- Prepare a list of options and send for brochures and a directory of Homes in your area.

- Familiarise the residents and relatives with the options. You may need to organise visits or use pictures. Be prepared to arrange for extra transport and staff.

- Prepare the potential receiving Homes to be welcoming.

- Arrange exchange visits of staff and proprietors or managers.

- Brief the receiving staff on the process at your end.

- Hold a formal review with each resident, with an advocate or relative present if necessary, to record individual needs and preferences.

- Designate a link person from your Home to approach a potential receiving Home to check the feasibility of admission.

- Draw up a checklist of each resident's care plan and other needs, for discussion over the transfer period.

- Confirm to residents and relatives in writing when a new placement has been arranged.

- Agree a procedure in case of a breakdown in a new placement. This is where the advice and help of an advocate will be very helpful. Also keep in touch with the advocate and relatives in case of a 'let down' factor (where a resident gets less attention in a new Home) or the opposite, where there is excessive euphoria in the early stages of a new placement.

- Prepare a receiving Home for possible resentment from their own residents, especially if several of your residents are transferring to the same Home.

- Clarify at an early stage the funding arrangements with the DSS or local authority, if necessary.

Staff

The procedure for dealing with your staff will depend very much on the contract agreements you have with them. However, even if you have no legal obligations, it will help you to maintain their loyalty during the crucial period before closure if you are seen to be doing all you can to help them.

- Research any options or entitlement as early as possible.

- Consider approaching other sectors in residential or domiciliary care (private, voluntary and local authority) in finding new jobs for your staff.

- Link up with local Job Centres.

- Try to phase staff departures to keep the Home appropriately staffed and to maintain continuity. Avoid using agency staff if possible. It may be preferable to bring in temporary staff for the whole closure period. You must always have minimum staffing levels as specified by the inspection and registration team. Consult them if you have problems.

- Emphasise to staff the benefits of security until closure to staff, to forestall premature departure.

- If you know where staff are moving to, prepare them and the new Home for a different work culture and style of operating.

- Attempt to maintain links between key workers or care staff and residents for a period after closure.

- Consider funding the 'new' Home to release your former staff occasionally to visit 'old' residents who have moved elsewhere.

- Consider the possibilities of paying retired or redundant staff to stay in close contact with former residents until the end of the review period (see below).

Review or follow-up

■ After the new placement, aim to have some kind of follow-up visits to your former residents at regular intervals, ideally at 4, 12 and 26 weeks from transfer. If possible, in between these times, arrange for a key worker or case worker to visit informally.

■ Involve the resident's family or advocate in the follow-up.

■ Clarify who is responsible and financially accountable in the event of a placement breakdown during or after the review period.

KEY POINTS

■ Start planning for closure at least six months before it will happen, if possible.

■ Set up a committee to co-ordinate the closure.

■ Inform staff and residents sensitively.

■ Bear in mind that some people will find it hard to take in the facts.

■ Be prepared for an emotional reaction.

■ Remember that the more you prepare, the easier it will be for you.

■ Check out alternative Homes and funding options as early as possible.

Green Fields

HOME CARE SERVICE

We are a husband and wife team who, in 1985, founded Ocean View House in Anytown as a comfortable home for elderly people. We have successfully combined the skills obtained from lifetime careers of nursing and hospital management on one hand with business management on the other to provide a professionally managed care service.

We have never lost sight of the OCEAN VIEW written philosophy which states:

'We believe that a safe and comfortable, dignified and caring environment is the right of all older people.

'We believe that economic services can be provided based on agreed conditions and standards to achieve these aims. Our clients will be consulted about their wishes, and they will at all times be treated with respect and a positive and pleasant manner.'

about Green Fields

Having established Ocean View House as a permanent home for older people and a holiday and convalescent relief service, we found that some of our clients wanted more flexibility. They were asking to come back on a day care basis from time to time, to give both themselves and their carers a break. This would also give them the opportunity to take advantage of the assisted bathing and other facilities provided at Ocean View House. We have been pleased to help and now offer day care as part of our Home Care Service 'menu'.

On other occasions, when our beds were full, help at home was requested. Again we were glad to help when an older person was alone or feeling off colour. We provided personal care, cleaning and cooked meals, organised minor maintenance work and checked security. This set us thinking: if our regular clients need help, they know whom to call. Are there others who need this service?

Green Fields Home Care *is only a phone call away!*

GREEN FIELDS

Home Care service for Retired Persons

If you need someone like us at a reasonable cost phone 0000-000 0000

Who can

▶ **make your bed**

▶ **cook your lunch**

▶ **wash or bath you**

▶ **dust and clean the house**

▶ **fix the drains**

▶ **sweep the path**

▶ **feed the cat**

▶ **walk the dog**

▶ **help you to bed**

▶ **take you shopping**

▶ **cut the grass**

▶ **do your washing**

▶ **wash your hair**

▶ **make a cup of tea and listen to your problems**

▶ **help you dress and more**

and smile while they do it.

Appendix 3

SUMMARY OF A LOCAL AUTHORITY CONTRACT

The summary given below is drawn from the documents that Oxfordshire County Council sends out to its potential providers of domiciliary care/assistance services. Other local authorities may have different individual requirements but all will include the same general specifications.

Conditions of contract

The document starts with an eighteen-page contract which covers 21 points in detail. The first part includes:

- the form and duration of the contract
- SSD contacts: authorised officer and/or care manager
- the service provider's obligations
- variation of services or additional services which may be required for a particular client
- staffing levels, and requirements for the proper levels of care, by both full-time and part-time employees
- control and supervision of staff.

The contract then sets out what will happen if there is default in performance, details of charges and payments, the rules on sub-contracting services, notice and arbitration.

Points to look out for

Obviously all sections should be studied carefully but providers should be particularly aware of their legal obligations under the contract. The clauses below, for instance, give many more powers to the authorised officer/care manager than an inspector has when inspecting a residential Home that has catered in the past purely for privately funded residents.

'**4.1.1** The service Provider shall provide the services in accordance with each Service Provision Plan in a proper, skillful and worklike manner, to the contract Standard and to the satisfaction of the Authorised Officer or Care Manager as the case may be.

'**4.1.2** The Service Provider shall ensure that each Care Worker is familiar with the requirements of the Service Provision Plan for the Client being provided with the services.

'**8.1** The Authorised Officer shall be entitled to take steps to ascertain whether the Service Provider has performed the Services and that he has done so in complete accordance with the Contract.'

Schedules

The rest of the document is taken up with Schedules, which set out in detail the authority's requirements in six areas:

- Specification of services
- Schedules of contract and travelling rates
- Policy on combined community health and social care
- Hygiene policy
- Safe food-handling requirements
- Drugs policy.

Points to look out for

As with the contract, it is up to providers to make sure that they can actually implement all the very detailed requirements under their current systems. It is important to estimate very carefully further costs in providing care before going ahead with local authority work. Some particular areas of difficulty may be:

- extra paperwork
- more stringent methods for handling food
- liaising with the district nurses and other health or social services professionals on behalf of each client
- training and monitoring and reviewing the work of staff.

Appendix 4

DUAL REGISTRATION

All nursing homes must be registered with the district health authority (DHA). If you are thinking about setting up a nursing area or wing in a residential Home, you must apply for dual registration. The local DHA will have guidelines on their particular requirements which you should go through carefully. As with inspection of a residential Home, the DHA will make sure that the manager (as well as the staff) has the right experience and qualifications to provide the appropriate level of nursing care, and that facilities are in place for this. Although it is not at present mandatory to have a separate nursing zone for patients, this is considered much the best practice and may be a requirement in the future.

Dual registration may attract higher funding, but it will also involve the Home owner in more intensive staffing and greater expenditure. Some of the main implications are:

- There must be a registered general nurse (RGN) on duty at all times, including the night. Sleeping in while on call is not allowed.

- The registering authority may refuse to register an applicant on the grounds of lack of managerial experience or the lack of experience with the client group, or if the applicant's qualifications are not appropriate to the client group.

- If residents not classified as being in need of nursing care become ill, they may receive that care only under the direction of a district nurse, even though there is a registered nurse on the premises.

The DHA registration officer will also check that the nursing home element of the Home is run with proper regard to the quality of care given to the patient. The following are based on points in the National Patient Charter Standard and the UKCC (UK Central Council for Nursing, Midwifery and Health Visiting) Code of Principles for Practice:

- The nursing Home should be run in such a way that patients can retain their personal dignity and maximum independence, taking into account the limitations of their physical or mental infirmity.

- A full pre-admission assessment should be made of each patient by a senior nurse member of the nursing Home staff. If possible, there should be a trial period for the patient and/or relative to assess the Home's suitability.

- The patient's health and psycho-social needs should be identified, as well as their abilities. A care plan should be written by the patient's named nurse, who will review the patient's health and condition regularly and revise the care plan accordingly.

Glossary

advocate A person appointed to represent someone who is not able to speak on their own account.

agency This is a catch-all term used to describe any number of public or private bodies. In the context of this book, it is used to describe a business that provides only care or nursing services and not residential care.

arm's length A term used to define the role of local authority inspection units which are an independent part of the SSD.

block contract A contract issued by the SSD for fixed-term or fixed-volume residential or domiciliary care.

care assistant A care worker in a residential Home.

care managers Social services workers who are responsible for assessing needs and drawing up care packages with user and carers; they then arrange for the provision of care services from the independent sector or from the local authority. Care managers purchase all independent services but may not have to budget for those provided by the local authority.

care package The combination of care services arranged by the purchaser.

carer A private individual who cares for an older person in their own home.

client The person who is paying for a service, who may be an individual or the SSD.

commissioning contracting unit The SSD department responsible for drawing up contracts for residential or domiciliary care.

diversification The process of finding new areas of business from the base of a residential Home.

domiciliary care Social or personal care in the context of an older person's own home.

dual registration Registration to enable a Home to provide both nursing and ordinary residential care in the same premises.

enabler A purchaser who arranges for care from outside their own agency or authority.

franchise system Operating a business under the 'umbrella' of a corporation that gives support as well as requiring certain standards of its franchisee.

home care Domiciliary care – a more user-friendly term.

independent sector A term used to describe all providers of care that operate for profit, not-for-profit voluntary organisations, housing associations and NHS Trusts.

individual contract A one-off contract for an older person's residential care.

inspection and registration unit The unit of the local authority responsible for inspecting and registering all independent residential Homes.

Investors in People (IIP) A new initiative designed to promote quality services, based on NVQs.

negative equity Where the financial commitment exceeds the value of the assets.

NVQs National Vocational Qualifications, achieved through training and practice on the job.

personal care Care of the person, eg bathing, dressing, lifting, giving food and drink.

preferred providers Providers (suppliers) whom the SSD believe will always deliver quality care and so will be among the first to be asked to provide care.

private sector Residential Homes and agencies that operate solely for profit.

provider The establishment that provides residential or domiciliary care.

purchaser The role of the care managers or commissioners in buying in care or care packages from the independent sector.

quality circle A meeting of people involved in one aspect of a business; for example, one director of a large public company holds regular quality circle meetings with his/her driver and personal assistant. The purpose of the meeting is to improve the way something is done and all opinions are equally valid. It is an excellent way of enabling staff to feel that their advice is welcomed and considered seriously.

SNVQs Scottish National Vocational Qualifications.

social care Help around the house, day or night sitting, conversation, taking for a drive, etc.

spot contract An SSD contract for a specific service or occasion, usually for one client.

SSD The local authority social services department.

STG Special Transitional Grant. Money transferred to local authorities from the Income Support budget for the purchase of care after April 1993. This grant ceases in 1996.

team briefing Discussion and briefing meeting held before major decisions are taken and implemented.

TECs Regional Training and Enterprise Councils.

user The person who actually receives services, whether or not they pay for them personally.

USP Unique selling point.

voluntary sector Organisations such as housing trusts or Age Concern England which are charities and non-profit making, though they may charge for their service.

Useful Addresses

City and Guilds Institute
46 Britannia Street
London WC1 9RG
Tel: 0171-278 9460

Hospice Information Service
51–59 Lawrie Park Road
Sydenham
London SE26 6DZ
Tel: 0181-778 9252

**Joint Advisory Group of
Domiciliary Care Associations**
c/o Lesley Bell
JICC Ltd
6 Minerva Gardens
Wyvendon Gate
Milton Keynes MK7 7SR
Tel: 01908 585373

**National Council for Vocational
Qualifications**
222 Euston Road
London NW1 2BZ
Tel: 0171-387 9898

**National Council for Voluntary
Organisations (NCVO)**
Regents Wharf
8 All Saints Street
London N1 9RL
Tel: 0171-713 6161

The Relatives Association
5 Tavistock Place
London WC1H 9SS
Tel: 0171-916 6055

Rural Development Commission
11 Cowley Street
London SW1P 3NA
Tel: 0171-276 6969

**United Kingdom Home Care
Association**
Premier House
Watson Mill lane
Sowerby Bridge
West Yorkshire HX6 3BW
Tel: 01422 835058

Also talk to local organisations

Training and Enterprise Council
(TEC)
Chamber of Commerce
Banks – Small Business
Departments
Colleges
Distance learning establishments

Further Reading

Books and packs

Care of Elderly People: the developing market for nursing and residential homes and related services in Britain (annual) Laing and Buisson Publications, London.

Caring for People – Information pack for the voluntary and private sectors (1993) Department of Health, London.

Caring for Quality in Day Services (1992) Department of Health, Social Services Inspectorate; HMSO, London.

Community Care Support Force – Stimulating diversification in the independent sector (1993) KPMG Peat Marwick, London.

Costing for Contracts: A practical guide for voluntary organisations (1992) NCVO, Directory of Social Change, London.

Developing Quality Standards for Home Support Services (1993) Department of Health, Social Services Inspectorate; HMSO, London.

Diversification and the Independent Residential Care Sector (1993), Department of Health, Social Services Inspectorate; HMSO, London.

The Empty Raincoat – Making sense of the future (1994) by Charles Handy, Hutchinson, London.

The Entrepreneur's Self-Assessment Guide – How to determine your potential for success (1987) by Douglas A Gray; Kogan Page, London.

Homes are for Living In (1989) Department of Health, Social Services Inspectorate; HMSO, London.

How to Market Care in Homes (1992) by Niamh Sreenan and Jef Smith, Counsel and Care, London.

Inspecting for Quality – Guidance on standards for short term breaks (1993) Department of Health, Social Services Inspectorate; HMSO, London

Laing's Review of Private Health Care, Laing and Buisson Publications, London.

Managing Change and Making it Stick (1987) by Roger Plant; Fontana, London.

Purchase of Service – Practice guidance and practice material for Social Services Departments and other agencies (1991) Department of Health, Social Services Inspectorate; HMSO, London.

Standards for Domiciliary Care (1992) Joint Advisory Group of Domiciliary Care Associations.

UKHCA Starter Pack, available from John Womersley, Homecarers, 14 Ledcamerock Road, Bearsden, Glasgow G61 4AB.

What Color is Your Parachute? (annual) Richard Nelson Bolles, Ten Speed Press.

Magazines and newspapers

Care Weekly, obtainable through newsagents.

Impact, NCVO Community Care Newspaper, published six times a year.

About Age Concern

Expanding Care – A practical guide to diversification for care homes is one of a wide range of publications produced by Age Concern England, the National Council on Ageing. Age Concern England is actively engaged in training, information provision, fundraising and campaigning for retired people and those who work with them, and also in the provision of products and services, such as insurance, for older people.

A network of over 1,400 local Age Concern groups, with the support of around 250,000 volunteers, aim to improve the quality of life for older people and develop services appropriate to local needs and resources. These include advice and information, day care, visiting services, transport schemes, clubs, and specialist facilities for older people who are physically and mentally frail.

Age Concern England is a registered charity dependent on public support for the continuation and development of its work.

Age Concern England
1268 London Road
London SW16 4ER
Tel: 0181-679 8000

Age Concern Cymru
4th Floor
1 Cathedral Road
Cardiff CF1 9SD
Tel: 01222 371566

Age Concern Scotland
54a Fountainbridge
Edinburgh EH3 9PT
Tel: 0131-228 5656

Age Concern Northern Ireland
3 Lower Crescent
Belfast BT7 1NR
Tel: 01232 245729

Publications from ◆◆◆ Books

A wide range of titles is published by Age Concern England under the ACE Books imprint.

Professional Handbook series

Taking Good Care: A handbook for care assistants
Jenyth Worsley
Written for professional carers of older people, this book covers such vital issues as the role of the care assistant in a residential home, communication skills, the medical and social problems encountered by carers, the resident's viewpoint and activities and group work.
£6.95   0–86242–072–5

Good Care Management: A guide to setting up and managing a residential home
Jenyth Worsley
This companion volume to *Taking Good Care* has been written for care home proprietors and managers, present and prospective. Topics covered include setting up a home, contracts, budgetary planning, staff management and training, the management of care and quality control.
£9.95   0–86242–104–7

The Community Care Handbook: The new system explained
Barbara Meredith
The delivery of care in the community has changed dramatically as a result of recent legislation, and continues to evolve. Written by one of the country's foremost experts, this book explains in practical terms why the reforms were necessary, what they are, how they operate and who they affect.
£11.95   0–86242–121–7

Health and Care

Carefully: A handbook for home care assistants

Lesley Bell

Recent legislation places increasing emphasis on the delivery of care to older people in their own homes, thereby underlining the crucial role of home care assistants. This accessible guide provides practical advice on the day-to-day tasks assistants encounter and addresses such issues as legal responsibilities and emotional involvement.

£9.95   0–86242–129–2

Dementia Care: A handbook for residential and day care

Alan Chapman, Alan Jacques and Mary Marshall

The number of dementia sufferers requiring care is increasing continuously. Written to complement *Taking Good Care*, this practical guide for professional carers offers an understanding of the condition and provides advice on such issues as daily care, health maintenance, home design and staffing strategies.

£9.95   0–86242–128–4

Old Age Abuse: A new perspective

Edited by Mervyn Eastman

Old age abuse is an often neglected and overlooked phenomenon of our society. Bringing together leading experts in this field, the second edition of this title examines current knowledge about the prevalence and causes of abuse, its diagnosis and treatment and the training programmes which can be used to raise awareness of the issue.

Co-published with Chapman and Hall

£13.99   0412–484–20–X

Finding and paying for residential care

Marina Lewycka

Acknowledging that an older person needs residential care often represents a major crisis for family and friends. Feelings of guilt and betrayal invariably compound the difficulties faced in identifying a suitable care home and sorting out the financial arrangements. This book provides a practical step by step guide to the decisions which have to be made and the help which is available.

£5.95   0–86242–157–8

Managing Other People's Money

Penny Letts

Foreword by The Master of the Court of Protection

The management of money and property is usually a personal and private matter. However, there may come a time when someone else has to take over on either a temporary or a permanent basis. This book looks at the circumstances in which such a need could arise and provides a step-by-step guide to the arrangements which have to be made.

£5.95   0–86242–090–3

Health Care in Residential Homes

Dr Anne Roberts

With far more older people receiving care in their own homes as a result of the community care reforms, staff working in residential care settings are likely to encounter a greater concentration of residents with severe health problems. In a clear and straightforward fashion this book provides information on the common illnesses of later life and the medicines prescribed for their treatment and offers advice on what should be done in an emergency.

£14.95   0–86242–156–X

If you would like to order any of these titles, please write to the address below, enclosing a cheque or money order for the appropriate amount made payable to Age Concern England. Credit card orders may be made on 0181-679 8000.

Publications Unit
Age Concern England
PO Box 9
London SW16 4EX

INFORMATION FACTSHEETS

Age Concern England produces 33 factsheets on a variety of subjects. They include:

Factsheet 10 *Local authority charging procedures for residential and nursing home care*

Factsheet 11 *Preserved rights to Income Support for residential and nursing homes*

Factsheet 17 *Housing Benefit and Council Tax Benefit*

Factsheet 18 *A brief guide to money benefits*

To order factsheets

Single copies are available free on receipt of a 9″ × 6″ sae. If you require a selection of factsheets or multiple copies totalling more than five, charges will be given on request.

A complete set of factsheets is available in a ring binder at the current cost of £34, which includes the first year's subscription. The current cost for annual subscription for subsequent years is £15. There are different rates of subscription for people living abroad.

Factsheets are revised and updated throughout the year and membership of the subscription service will ensure that your information is always current.

For further information, or to order factsheets, write to:

Information and Policy Department
Age Concern England
1268 London Road
London SW16 4ER

Index